AFRICA'S WINDS
OF CHANGE

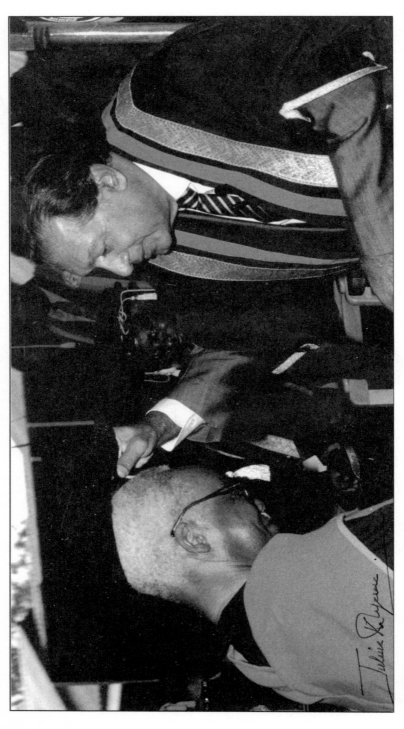

As Chancellor of Sokoine University of Agriculture, the author confers an honorary Doctor of Philosophy degree on the first Tanzanian President, Julius Nyerere, on 28 November 1997.

AFRICA'S WINDS OF CHANGE

Memoirs of an International Tanzanian

AL NOOR KASSUM

I.B. TAURIS

LONDON · NEW YORK

Published in 2007 by I.B.Tauris & Co Ltd
6 Salem Road, London W2 4BU
175 Fifth Avenue, New York NY 10010
www.ibtauris.com

In the United States of America and Canada distributed by Palgrave Macmillan
a division of St. Martin's Press, 175 Fifth Avenue, New York NY 10010

ISBN: 978 1 84511 583 8

A full CIP record for this book is available from the British Library
A full CIP record is available from the Library of Congress

Library of Congress Catalog Card Number: available

Printed and bound in Great Britain by TJ International Ltd, Padstow, Cornwall
From camera-ready copy edited and supplied by the author

I dedicate these memoirs
to Mama Maria Nyerere
for her devotion to Mwalimu
throughout his life

CONTENTS

FOREWORD

The late 1950s were critical and decisive years in the political developments that would lead to the independence of Tanganyika on 9 December 1961. Many leaders featured in the political groundwork for independence, within the nationalist movement represented by he Tanganyika African National Union, the Asian Association, and in individual communities and civil society. They were also destined to feature equally prominently in the first three decades of independence and the formation of the United Republic of Tanzania in 1964.

Among the towering figures in the Asian community can be counted Amir Habib Jamal, Mahmoud Rattansey – and Al Noor Kassum. These memoirs are a lean account of his life of sturdy, committed and productive service to his nation, Tanzania, and wholehearted loyalty to its founding father, the late President Mwalimu Julius K. Nyerere. I consider it lean because Nick, which is what he is called by friends and colleagues, has made a contribution to the building of the nation of Tanzania that should speak volumes.

It is doubtful that his parents had political ambitions for him; it is likely that political distinction and service was thrust upon him. His father migrated from India in the 1890s and started a grocery business which in due course grew in scope, coverage and prosperity. Although he was not very educated, he ensured that his children received an education – probably so that they could gravitate into business. In the event, Nick received his education in Tanganyika, India and the United Kingdom, finally being called to the Bar at Lincoln's Inn, London, and admitted to the Advocates' Roll in Dar es Salaam in 1954.

Those who have worked with him closely and satisfactorily but did not get to know him personally will find these memoirs replete with delightful revelations. How, for example, he changed his name by deed poll from Noordin ('light of religion') to Al Noor ('the light') because the late Aga Khan Sir Sultan Muhammad Shah, during His Highness' Diamond Jubilee celebrations, kept calling him Noor until the Begum Aga Khan, Mata Salamat, told him, 'Don't forget now, your name is Al Noor!' Or that, while studying in India he nearly joined the Intelligence Corps of the British Royal Air Force in India, so good was his English accent!

Al Noor Kassum has evinced a commanding passion for education and equality throughout his public life, well grounded in his academic high marks during his studies and legal training. As early as 1954, the Aga Khan appointed him Administrator of the Aga Khan schools in Tanganyika. His interest in education emerged more powerfully during his maiden speech in the Legislative Council to which he had been nominated in October 1958.

It was on what he himself described as his 'pet subject', namely, education. Opposing the segregated educational system then extant, with a European Education Authority, Indian Education Authority and African Advisory Committee, he called it 'an anachronism' and went on to say that all these resources should be pooled and secondary education in all of these schools made 'available to a person of ability, irrespective of his race, caste or creed or colour'. He made a plea to make 'our children think from this moment in terms of tolerance and charity'. The speech is in Chapter 2 and I wish it would be made compulsory reading for the youth of today. Mwalimu Nyerere was so moved by this speech that at the end of the proceedings he ran across the Chamber to him and asked, 'What on earth are you doing on that side of the House? You should join us and run for one of the Asian seats in next year's elections.' The following year he became the Member of Parliament for Dodoma. He sustained and promoted his interest in education in the following years, as Parliamentary Secretary for Education and Information.

Nick's love for and belief in his country, as well as his deep respect for Mwalimu Nyerere are well illustrated throughout the book. Upon the advent of nationalization, which saw the loss of the family's commercial property interests, he saw the move as an extension of TANU's creed of equality in all fields. He concedes that he 'was not sure what the future would bring to Tanzania'. Nevertheless, he wrote to Mwalimu thus: 'My love of and belief in Tanzania and my highest respect for you are such that I shall continue to do, to the extent of my ability, whatever I feel is in the interest of Tanzania and its people.'

Having worked with him as a colleague in the previous incarnation of the East African Legislative Assembly, the Tanzanian Parliament and Cabinet, I can attest to his breadth of profound intellect, managerial talent and diplomatic skills. These can be easily discerned in his account of his tenure as Deputy General Manager of Williamson Diamonds Ltd, as Minister of Finance and Administration of the East African Community, and Tanzania Minister for Water, Energy and Minerals. His disposition to probe, to listen, to diagnose and to reconcile divergent views, to strategize implementation of decisions and to superintend accountability, is rivetingly illuminated in Chapters 5, 6 and 7. Present legislators, politicians and academicians would benefit immensely were they to read therein about the currently contentious issues of ownership and management of public enterprises on the one hand and the fast-tracking of East African cooperation on the other!

Throughout our association I have admired Nick Kassum for his brilliant mind, his articulate tongue and his solicitous hand. His humour is catching and friendly. His criticism is disarming. He teases gently, always exuding warm empathy. He accepts praise with modesty but is exceedingly generous in his commendation of others. 'Writing is not a profession, but a vocation of unhappiness,' said George Simenon. I am delighted that, though retired, Nick decided temporarily to embark on the vocation of writing this book of memoirs. It is certain to give great happiness to his many friends. But, more importantly, it is bound to enrich the history of Tanzania.

Benjamin William Mkapa

PREFACE

These memoirs have been difficult to write for two reasons. Firstly, I am not the sort of person who looks back on his life and counts his achievements. I believe that life should be lived as it comes and that every challenge should be tackled by making full use of one's capabilities. Secondly, no one can really judge his work in his lifetime. It is only those who come later who will be in a position to look objectively at the historical context and make a judgement.

Why, then, did I write these memoirs? It is because, over the years many friends and colleagues have been trying to persuade me to leave for posterity an account of the challenges that Tanzania faced from powerful global forces in the crucial early days of its development and the endeavours that were made against overwhelming odds to improve the lives of Tanzanians, as well as my own place in those endeavours. I have attempted to do this so that those who have not experienced that period in my country's history will gain an understanding of the steps that brought us to where we are today.

During the Cold War, any attempt by a country to develop without accepting external control was perceived as alliance with one of the superpowers, and this affected media and other reports about that country. Tanzania found itself in that situation, as a result of which many people received distorted impressions of its policies and actions. So one of the reasons for writing this book was also to correct some of the misapprehensions about Tanzania. In order to do so credibly, I have quoted extensively from correspondence as well as speeches. Sometimes I have given the speeches verbatim because they express the issues much more clearly than I would if I were to rephrase them today with different phrasing. I ask the reader to bear with me at such times.

Many people have contributed to writing this book, but none more so than my loving wife Yasmin, who has supported me in all my endeavours. Particularly in the last 10 to 15 years, she has witnessed some of the events which are part of these memoirs.

I am also grateful to Amin Kassam for the long hours he devoted to the project, from the first raw data to the final manuscript. We spent much time together discussing what to include and how to present it, and though we sometimes disagreed, the process created a strong bond of friendship between us. Because of his professional background as an editor, he was able to help me in my style, grammar, terminology and so on. I am heavily indebted to Kutub Kassam for the highly professional input that he has provided in every chapter of the book with in-depth analysis that could only have been done by someone of his calibre. I am truly, truly grateful to him because, as a result, I have learnt a great deal, too. In addition, I am deeply grateful to my dear friend Mohamed M. Keshavjee of South Africa and Kenya. A keen student of this period of Africa's history, he spurred me on to write about my work for my country. He constantly reminded me of how important it was for future generations of Tanzanians in the diaspora to gain an insight into the interesting developments that took place during the years of my experience. To help me realize this, he spent numerous hours with me in Nairobi, Dar es Salaam, and Chantilly, France, contributing selflessly to this endeavour. Of course, while these memoirs gained enormously from his insights, I take full responsibility for everything in them.

Ultimately, this book has been stimulated by my love for Tanzania and my deep admiration and respect for Mwalimu Julius Kambarage Nyerere, the architect of this country's independence as well as its first President, and the many colleagues with whom I worked in the Government as well as in international institutions.

Al Noor Kassum

1

EARLY YEARS IN TANGANYIKA AND ABROAD

My first memory of Mwalimu Julius Kambarage Nyerere, the man who has played a very significant role in my life, is that of a calm person who used to come shopping at my father's grocery store in Dar es Salaam. At that time, he was a teacher in the village of Pugu, not far from Dar es Salaam, and no one could have foretold that he would one day be President of Tanganyika (which would later unite with Zanzibar to form Tanzania) and one of the most respected statesmen in Africa.

I met him again a decade later, in the early 1950s, when we were both studying in Britain. I was studying law at Lincoln's Inn and, like other East African students in London, visited East Africa House at Marble Arch from time to time to catch up on the news from the continent. Mwalimu was studying for a Master of Arts at Edinburgh University and was in London for a few days during which he turned up at Marble Arch.

'Hello, I am from Tanganyika,' I said, putting out my hand. 'I remember you,' said Julius Nyerere, and we shook hands. We conversed a little and parted. I still had no inkling then of the important role that Mwalimu was to play later in my life.

* * * *

I doubt that my parents had political ambitions for me when I was young. My father, Kassum Sunderji Samji, had been born into an Ismaili Muslim family of dairy farmers in Jamnagar district, Gujarat, western India. At that time there was a heavy migration of people from western India to eastern and southern parts of Africa. In 1896 my father accompanied his parents and some other members of the family when they migrated to Tanganyika. Two years previously, Britain, then the major global imperial power, had agreed to let Germany have a sphere of influence over that East African territory, except for a 10-mile-wide strip of land along the coast, which was to be ruled by the Sultan of Zanzibar. Although Dar es Salaam was under the Sultan's authority, many Germans lived there.

When my father arrived in Tanganyika, it was with the intention of being a dairy farmer. However, he soon decided to break with family tradition and go into trade. At the age of 15 years, he found employment as a shop assistant/clerk with a German company called Max Stephens. Over about seven years, he learned the ins and outs of trade as well as the German language. (He became so fluent in German that by the time he died in 1974, he spoke it better than any other language.) After the First World War broke out in 1914, the German owner of the company returned home. My father then opened his own shop on Acacia Avenue (now Samora Avenue), a part of Dar es Salaam where the majority of the European population lived and traded. Some of the government offices were also on this street.

My father imported and sold a wide range of goods: tinned foods (for example, beans and sardines), fresh fruits from South Africa, wines from France, spirits, cheeses of various kinds, cigarettes and tobacco from Britain and elsewhere, almost everything that his customers wanted. He had agents in various countries. His agent in Britain was a man named I. Gundle, whose son Aubrey was later to be like a guardian to me while I was at school in England. The shop did well and my father built another, much bigger, grocery store, also named Kasssum's Store, farther along Acacia Avenue. The name is still discernible on the building in modern-day Dar es Salaam. It was to this shop that Mwalimu Julius Nyerere used to come when he was a teacher in Pugu. Most of the government officials, including the Governor, did their shopping there. With the profits from his grocery business, my father gradually bought up all the properties surrounding it, and after improvement and further development of buildings, he rented them out. I was born in the family residence above the shop.

From this small beginning, my father's business grew into one of the largest and best-stocked grocery stores in East Africa. Many family members worked in the shop, including my older brother Hassanali. While my father was the overall 'boss', the shop was managed on a day-to-day basis by my maternal uncle, Alibhai Abdullah Ratansi. My uncle also handled the financial aspects of the business, assisted by my brother Hassanali, since my father had no formal education and could hardly write. The customers were mostly European. After the League of Nations gave Britain a mandate over Tanganyika in 1919, the European population of Dar es Salaam increasingly became British, but there were other European nationalities as well.

Wealth did not make my father selfish and acquisitive, and he donated generously to charities. The school I attended in my childhood was built on land donated by him, as was one of the city's most modern hospitals. On one occasion, he donated a full set of brass band instruments to an African secondary school in Tabora, this at a time when communities of different races made donations only for the benefit of their own members. He was also very active in the affairs of the Ismaili Muslim community and was appointed President of the Ismailia Council for Tanganyika. In recognition of his service to the community, the title of 'Count' was conferred on him by the Ismaili Imam, the late Aga Khan III, Sir Sultan Muhammad Shah.

My memory of my father in the context of family life is also that of a kind and generous man. He used to become angry easily, but then he would make up for it very quickly, too. Although having had no formal education, he was an extraordinarily clever man, and that showed in everything he did. I learned two main lessons from my father and I have passed them on to my sons. First, that education is very important and that one should always do every job well. Second, that they should never antagonize anyone unnecessarily, and that generally they should be very charitable in helping others. My father was full of goodness and did 'the right thing' without thinking about it. He was able to mix with people of all types.

Because of his wealth and charitable work, my father became quite influential and the then Governor, Sir Edward Twining, appointed him an unofficial nominated member of the Tanganyika Legislative Council. He was one of four Asian members. The others were Dr. S.B. Malik, D.K. Patel and A.A.A. Adamjee. My father was a member of the Legislative Council from 1936 to 1940. However, even then, as an Asian, he was not allowed to enter a hotel set aside for Europeans. He was also not allowed to live in European areas. Eventually this regulation was circumvented when my father joined with some other

Asians in buying land for salt pans at Oyster Bay. When he could afford it, he bought out his partners. The government realized at that time that he owned a large piece of land in a European area and it agreed to let him keep one parcel of the land if he would give the rest up to the government. In this way, he became the first Asian to be allowed to have a house in Oyster Bay, although it took some time before he could actually live in it. In the late 1930s and early 1940s it was occupied by the British and used as a convalescent home for servicemen, particularly from the Royal Air Force. Later, we moved into the house. Since then, all members of the Aga Khan's family have stayed at the house at one time or another.

My father was as unorthodox in his choice of wife as he was in his choice of career. He married Sikina, daughter of Abdullah Ratansi of Zanzibar. What made the marriage unusual was that Sikina's parents were from Kutch in India, while my father's parents were Nangaria (people from Jamnagar). Marriage between the two groups, even if the couple were Ismailis, was frowned upon and practically unheard of at that time. This was probably due to local customary caste differences in that part of India. However, today even interracial and interfaith marriages are generally accepted among the Ismaili Muslims everywhere.

I was born on 11 January 1924, the second of three sons. The eldest was Hassanali, nicknamed Chocolate. The youngest brother was Kamruddin and he is better known as Ken. My mother also gave birth to three daughters: Sakar Bai, Nurkhanu and Rosy. I was about five years old when Hassanali got married. As part of the ceremony, he rode on a white horse in a procession from our home to the bride's family home. Because I had reached male maturity, I also rode on a pony behind him. It was the first time I had ever ridden a horse, but I was too excited to be frightened. I can still remember the swirl of the crowds, the bands, the fireworks, and the colourful dresses. Only the wealthy could afford weddings of such splendour. It was a time when we lived in a world of our own and nothing intruded into it. It was only as I grew older that I became conscious that not only were there different races, but that each race had been allocated its own place in Tanganyikan society.

In 1933, my mother died of pregnancy complications about half an hour after giving birth to my brother Ken. I was then nine years old. My mother and I had been very close. She expressed her love for me in many ways, but the one I remember most was how she served me peanuts, which were a particularly favourite food of mine. She would shell the peanuts and then pound them into a paste, which she would give me to eat. I cherished that paste and valued it far above all the fancy chocolates and other foods available to me in our shop downstairs.

I enjoyed living in Dar es Salaam. I went several times to Zanzibar with my brother Hassanali when he was visiting his in-laws and I found it a beautiful place. We travelled for five shillings in a boat named *Dumra*. The journey to Zanzibar island took five to six hours and the salty taste and tingle of the ocean breeze was a joy. Zanzibar was richer than Dar es Salaam, not just in terms of money derived from its spice trade with the outside world, but also because of its natural resources. The fruits had a richer taste, the smell of cloves that permeated the island was exhilarating. The tangy Indian snacks, such as *bhajias*, tasted much better there than in Dar es Salaam. However, had my family decided to move to Zanzibar I would have missed
Dar es Salaam's own unique ambience that made it home for me.

As the son of a wealthy man, I had a fairly easy life. Every morning I was taken to school in a rickshaw, while most of my fellow pupils had to walk. My time outside school was spent going to the mosque, playing cricket, flying kites, playing marbles and attending music parties, among other things. On Sundays the whole family would pile into the family car and go for a drive around Dar es Salaam and along the ocean front. At that time, the education system in Tanganyika was based on race: Africans, Asians and Europeans had their own, separate schools. The law forbade interracial schools. Moreover, each Asian community established its own schools, although the British administration did establish a few schools specifically for Asians. In the non-European schools, education standards were different from those in Britain. My teachers mostly came from India. To this day, when I am calculating something mentally, I do so on the basis of the multiplication tables I learned by heart in Gujarati because that was the language of instruction in the school. (I can still remember the canings I received when I did not learn my tables properly!) The subjects were limited: besides Gujarati, a little arithmetic, geography and history of the British Empire, and religion. There were 30 to 40 children per class. In this context, it was not surprising that, in 1934, after the death of my mother, desirous of giving me a good start in life, my father decided to send me to a boarding school in England. Later I realized it was the best gift he could have given me.

Communications then were not as simple as they are today, and a trip to England for me was like a trip to another planet. My father (who was going to Europe to meet the late Aga Khan as well as on business) and I went by a Messageries Maritime ship, *Le Conte de l'Isle*, accompanied by several other prominent Ismailis, who were also travelling to England for their own reasons. Among them were Count Jindani accompanied by his two daughters; Suleman Virjee; and Varas Mohammed Saleh Kanji from Zanzibar. We sailed to Marseilles, where we had a first meeting with the late Aga Khan. (Later, we met His Highness again in London, with other members of the Ismaili community.) We were received very warmly and it was a joyful occasion for all of us. Then, we went by train to Calais, from where we sailed to Dover and then travelled again by train to London.

In England, for the first time I was in a society where I was a curiosity. I could almost see people thinking, 'Where is he from?' While I was used to Europeans in Dar es Salaam, I had never been in a country where there were so many of them – in the streets, on the buses, in cars, and in shops. Asians were then rare in England and it made me realize how different my life was going to be.

My father enrolled me at Muncaster School in Ashford, Middlesex. It was a small school, with about 80 to 90 pupils. Four other Ismaili boys from East Africa were also enrolled there: Saleh Mohammed Saleh Kassam; Gaverally Gulamhussein Abdullah Shariff; and two brothers, Ali Jessa Bhaloo and Hussain Jessa Bhaloo. Although Muncaster was a boys' school, Count Jindani managed to enrol his two daughters Guly and Meera there for a term, so that they could get acclimatized while having East Africans around them before being transferred to a girls' school. The three other Ismaili boys were withdrawn from the school by their parents within a few months, leaving me the sole non-white pupil. After I had been there three years, a distant cousin of the Sultan of Zanzibar joined the school, but he left within a short time apparently because he was unable to adapt to the egalitarian life of a boarding school.

The momentum towards the Second World War was building while I was at Muncaster, but I enjoyed my school days. I could speak just a few words of English when I arrived, so communication during the first weeks involved a lot of gestures. The headmaster,

David McWilliams, who also owned the school, was patient, as were the teachers and my fellow pupils, and I quickly picked up the language. Looking back, I can see that it was an advantage to learn the language from scratch: I did not have an accent to overcome. The headmaster and teachers took pains to ensure that I felt at home. I particularly liked sports and eventually became captain of the cricket and football teams. I was also appointed a senior prefect.

My father felt that a knowledge of typing and shorthand would be essential for my future. Therefore, when dropping me off at the school, he had asked the headmaster to arrange for me to take lessons in these subjects. Muncaster did not teach typing and shorthand, so I had to go outside the school for those lessons. I am afraid I was not a good typist and the squiggles of shorthand did not appeal to me. I have often thought what a pity it was that my father did not consider playing the piano an essential skill, for I would have loved to learn that!

Every morning at the school, the pupils congregated in the assembly hall to listen to readings from the Bible. We took turns to read out passages from the Bible and one day it was my turn to do so. I read out a passage and later explained that, while, as a non-Christian, I was not fully conversant with all the meanings of the passage I had read out, ultimately we all believed in the same God. This is a belief that has stayed with me throughout my life. I look at people as individuals, not in terms of their religion. People should be free to believe in whatever religion they want and to express that belief. Belief in God, in whatever religious context, should be a factor uniting people, not dividing them. At the same time, I am doubtful about the feasibility of hermetically dividing the religious from the secular in everyday life in order to avoid religious discord, as is being proposed in some quarters these days. It merely hurts and creates resentment. Instead, society should let the process of concord evolve naturally.

One of my special friends at Muncaster was Henry Stanley, a day boy, who used to take me home with him sometimes. Another friend was Henry Zollschan, a Jew of Hungarian origin whose parents had migrated to France. After I left the school we exchanged greeting cards occasionally, but we lost contact soon after the Second World War. Then there was Henry Walter, also a day boy. During a visit to his home I was introduced to his sister Marie, who was about the same age as me, and we all became good friends.

During the long summer holidays, teachers would invite me in turn to stay for a month at their homes. I recall sojourns in Liverpool, Brighton, Dorset and Cardiff. In Dorset I swam a lot with other children of my age and rambled through the downs, collecting flowers. I made many friends, not in the homes of my teachers but outside, in the villages. When I went to Cardiff, I visited a coal mine and met a lot of young workers there. It was a harsh occupation. I met many people during the holidays and we became great friends. They liked to exploit my ignorance and I did the same to them.

I never encountered any form of overt racism at the school. However, outside the school premises it was a different story. I was going through my adolescence and becoming very interested in the opposite sex. Initially, my attempts to chat with girls resulted in retorts such as 'you nigger', 'darkee' and 'inkee', and I was told to 'go back home'. But I persisted and after a while they became very friendly.

Muncaster School was moved to Laleham-on-Thames, near Staines, after the outbreak of the Second World War. The potential horror of war was brought home to me on 3 September 1939, as I was out cycling near Windsor with a friend and we heard people saying that London had been bombed. We rushed back to school, to find that the rumour was false. However, the headmaster told the pupils that air raids were, indeed, a possibility in future. By November, my father decided that I would be safer in Dar es Salaam and called me back home. This was a disappointment to me because I had fully prepared myself for the London matriculation exams, which all my teachers expected me to pass. I had to leave for home in December without sitting the exams, but carried letters from my teachers to the effect that I would have passed the exams if I had sat for them. This time I travelled by flying boat (the last one to Tanganyika after the declaration of war) and the journey from Southampton to Dar es Salaam, via France, Italy, Corfu, Egypt, Sudan and Kenya, took eight days. We flew only during the day, the nights being spent at various stopovers along the way.

During an overnight halt in the Kenyan town of Kisumu, on the shores of Lake Victoria, I was told that the founder of the Boy Scouts movement, Lord Baden Powell, was staying at the same hotel. He was easily recognisable in his Scout uniform and I introduced myself to him, telling him I had been a cub scout in Dar es Salaam. I was so excited at meeting the great man that I do not remember now what else I said or his replies. I recalled the thrill of that meeting again many years later, when, after national independence, I was appointed Chairman of the Scout Council in Dar es Salaam for two years.

On my return from England, I met my stepmother for the first time. My father had married again while I was at school. My stepmother was Remtibai Gulamhussein Abdulhussein, the sister of Count A.G. Abdulhussein, President of the Ismailia Council in Tanganyika (a position which my father had also once held). She gave birth to two sons, Navroz and Sultan, and a daughter, Fatma. We all became quite close and I persuaded my father to send them for education to England as well.

After my return from England, I joined my father's business. My working day started at around 8 a.m. The shop was shut during lunchtime, which was from half-past noon to 2 p.m., and then back in the shop till closing time at 6 p.m. (I sometimes left earlier, to play tennis.) As a customer entered the shop, on the right-hand side he would see a display of confectionery of various types: chocolates from Switzerland and Britain, toffee, peppermints, sugar almonds, everything to satisfy a sweet tooth. Then came biscuits of all kinds, plain, chocolate covered, sugared, digestive, ginger nuts. On the opposite shelves were wines and spirits. Further in the shop was the fresh food section: hams, cheeses and other perishables. At the back were the tinned foods. The air was lightly redolent with the smell of spices, which were sold in sealed tins but somehow managed to spread their aroma throughout the shop. There were also dried fruits such as figs, prunes and apricots, and many types of nuts. The shelves were a forest of different colours, depending upon the packaging of each product. When the customers – who were almost all white – entered, they would be approached by a salesman who would serve them. Most of the customers were women wearing colourful knee-length dresses, and they came in cars, which were parked outside the shop, and were mostly accompanied by a servant carrying a basket for the purchases. Male customers, wearing white or khaki short-sleeved shirts, shorts and stockings, came mainly to buy tobacco and drinks.

For a teenager, the shop was a paradise, with every day bringing new experiences, and I found the work pleasurable. But my father was already planning a different future for me.

2

FROM LINCOLN'S INN TO LEGISLATIVE COUNCIL

My father was not happy about my joining his business at such a young age and wanted me to get some sort of professional training. Next door to the grocery store, in a building owned by my father, was a radio shop called Souza Junior Dias (Radio) Ltd, in which he had a 50 per cent shareholding. That gave him the idea that radio engineering would be a useful skill for me to learn. My father's friends suggested that India would be a suitable place for such training, so in February1941 I set off for Bombay on a British India ship named S.S. Karagola.

In Bombay, I was met by an Ismaili merchant named Gulamali Chunara, one of my father's business contacts, who took me to stay at the YMCA on Lemmington Road. I enrolled for a radio engineering course at Fazalbhai Technical Institute in St Xavier's College, but I found that I did not like radio engineering and gave it up after six months. I then joined Batliboi's Technical Institute, where I learned double-entry book-keeping and how to draw up simple balance sheets. After six months I gave that up, too, and started buying goods for my father, mostly at the Mulji Jetha Market and other wholesalers.

Among the friends I made in Bombay was Bobby Padamsi, who had studied at Oxford University and noticed my English accent. We became close friends. He used to take me to his home, where I met his mother, brother and sisters. Another friend was Sultan Padamsi (not related to Bobby), who used to take me to his house in Juhu and we used to have picnics in that area. I was popular among the Ismaili students in Bombay and was elected Joint Secretary of the Ismailia Students' Association. I also joined the Indian Congress Party, which was leading the movement for independence from the British, but my motives were not political. Although I have served in many political positions, I have never been a political person. The positions have come to me not because I sought them, but because others have seen things in me that made them confident of my ability to do the job. Once in the job, I have always devoted all my attention to it and carried it out satisfactorily.

As a young man in India, although I was moved by the seething political atmosphere, I joined Congress only because it was the thing to do for people of my age. During a party, I once met Mohammed Ali Jinnah, who later, in 1947, became the founding father of Pakistan. I was greatly saddened when India was partitioned into two countries. Having seen different communities living together amicably during my stay in Bombay, I think it would have been much better for the people if the political leaders had negotiated a federation instead of splitting the subcontinent into separate, hostile countries.

I enjoyed going for coffee to the Taj Mahal Hotel and other similar places in the city. Two of my favourite areas in Bombay were Chaupati and the neighbourhood of the Empire Cinema, where I could get the most mouth-watering *bhel puri*. Those snacks of spiced chickpeas and condiments on a base of deep-fried unleavened dough were heavenly. I also liked going to Indian films and my favourite actress in those days was Lila Chitnis. I made a point of seeing the films in which she and Ashok Kumar starred. Indian films are chock-full of vibrant songs and that was perhaps why I started taking lessons in Indian music – ironically, from a White Father at St Xavier's College. My music lessons made me more appreciative of the beautiful intricacies of Indian *ragas*. I also played tennis, winning the doubles championship at St Xavier's College with a Parsi student named Russi Modi, who later became Managing Director of Air India. At the YMCA, Maharastrian girls used to come to play badminton and I would join them. The allowance I received from my father was more than that received by the other students, so I was able to enjoy life to the full and entertain friends on many occasions. My room at the YMCA was slightly larger than those of the others and I was able to buy additional furnishings for it.

My stay in Bombay strengthened my consciousness of Indian culture. Occasionally I ate my food from a metal plate called a *thali*, and for a week or two I even wore a *dhoti* (loin cloth) all the time. Whenever I went to the Mulji Jetha Market to buy things for my father, I used to wear either a *dhoti* or a *shalwar* (loose trousers made of thin cotton cloth) topped off with a *khamis* (loose tunic).

One of the highlights of my stay in Bombay was a meeting with Prince Aly Khan, the eldest son of the late Aga Khan and father of the present Imam. He used to visit Tanganyika quite often and on one occasion he and his wife, the film star Rita Hayworth, had stayed at my father's home in Oyster Bay. During Prince Aly Khan's visit to Bombay, two fellow East African Ismaili students and I called on him to pay our respects. The other two students were Kamruddin Shariff Pradhan and Abdul Tejpar.

When I had been in India for about 18 months, I applied for a commission as a junior officer in the British Royal Air Force in India. Once again, there was no political motive; I just thought it would be an interesting experience. About 400 applicants took the test in Bangalore. The moment the senior officers who were conducting the interviews heard my English accent, there was no doubt in their minds about my suitability. Without needing to prove my ability to do the job, I was selected to join the Intelligence Corps. I was instructed to report for training to a unit at Mhow near Poona. Predictably, as soon as news of my intentions reached the family home in Dar es Salaam, there was much concern. I received a telegram from my brother Hassanali reading, 'Father on his death bed. I suggest you come back and see him.' I returned to Dar es Salaam in August 1942 on the next available ship, the *SS Tilawa*, only to find my father well and healthy. Thus, because of my brother's ruse, I did not join the RAF. The voyage home was uneventful, but on the return journey to India the *SS Tilawa* was torpedoed by a Japanese submarine. Fortunately, of the 958 people aboard, many survived.

Whilst in Bombay, I had met Count V.M. Nazerally who was visiting India with his family, including his daughter Shirin whom I had met earlier in Dar es Salaam. On my return to Dar es Salaam on 30 June 1943, I married Shirin and we had our first child, Saleem, on 21 May 1944.

In Dar es Salaam, I once again began working in my father's grocery store. In 1947 India finally won its independence and the British found themselves with the problem of finding work for the soldiers who had to be withdrawn from the subcontinent. One of the solutions they came up was a groundnut scheme in the Mtwara and Kongwa areas of Tanganyika. The hundreds of soldiers participating in the project needed supplies and their purchasing officer, a Colonel Porter, came to us. His needs far outstripped our stocks, so I used to fly to Mombasa in Kenya, where I bought goods from a prominent Ismaili merchant, Count Fatehali Dhala, and his associates. I did much business supplying the British forces during this time.

At that time, Dar es Salaam had only two cinemas and, because the tickets were expensive, the audiences were usually the well-to-do. My brother Hassanali was fascinated by films and he and some business partners formed an enterprise called Indo-African Theatres Ltd. They had cinemas in Nairobi and Zanzibar. The partners were Harbanslal, a Punjabi from Nairobi; a Parsee named Talati from Zanzibar, who imported films from India; and Thawer, an Ismaili from Zanzibar. They also gave me some shares in the company. They suggested to my father that he build a cinema which they would then lease from him. Our family owned a godown that was leased by an Arab businessman named Yahya Mohammed, which was ideal for conversion into a cinema. After the businessman vacated the premises, I supervised the conversion of the building into the Avalon cinema, which was opened in 1944 by the Mayor of Dar es Salaam, Tom Tyrell. In addition to Indian films, we also screened films from the UK and USA. We imported the latest films and screened them for a week.

The cinema became very popular in Dar es Salaam. Even my father was drawn to it: after prayers at the mosque he would go and see whatever was being screened before returning home for dinner. Sometimes he would view the same film again on another evening. After some time he developed the property next to the cinema, and years later that was where I was to set up my first office as a lawyer.

Following the success of the Avalon, my father decided that the ticket prices were too high for the African population and he built a cinema called the Amana. It was part of a complex of shops and flats at Kariakoo in Ilala, where the majority of the Africans lived. Tickets at the Amana were priced at one-third those at the Avalon. That action was typical of my father. Even though he was wealthy, he was always thinking of how he could help less-fortunate people. The Amana cinema was opened by the Governor, Sir Edward Twining. The building still stands today, but has been converted into a youth centre.

In 1945, at the age of 21, I was appointed a municipal councillor. I think the main reason for this was that most of the decision-makers shopped at my father's grocery store and could see for themselves that I had a very good command of English and that I was capable of contributing positively to the council's work. Both the Mayor and the Town Clerk were Englishmen, as were some of the councillors. I was elected Chairman of the Traffic, Fire and Lighting Committee and it was under my chairmanship that the current fire station on the road to the University of Dar es Salaam was constructed. During that time, I also became a Rotarian and was among the first non-whites to join the Round Table.

* * * *

One of the major events in my life occurred in 1946, with the Diamond Jubilee celebration of His Highness Sir Sultan Muhammad Shah's accession to the Imamat and thus his leadership of the Ismaili Muslim community worldwide. The celebration was marked by a ceremony that riveted the attention of people internationally: the Aga Khan visited various capitals, where the Ismailis demonstrated their love for him by weighing him in diamonds. The media were full of breathless stories about the event, to such an extent that its real nature was often distorted by the drama. For the Ismailis it was a symbolic ceremony to commemorate the sixtieth anniversary of the Aga Khan's Imamat, to express their devotion to him and appreciation of his leadership. In Dar es Salaam, the celebration was held in the grounds of the Ismaili *jamatkhana* in Upanga. Our family wanted to accommodate the Aga Khan at our Oyster Bay house, but it had not yet been returned to us. Therefore, we asked a tenant of another of our houses to vacate it for the Aga Khan. During the Aga Khan's visit to Dar es Salaam in the previous year, I had been asked to be His Highness' aide-de-camp, and that honour was given to me again for the Diamond Jubilee.

On the day of the Diamond Jubilee ceremony, wearing a red fez, I was seated on the steps of the dais, next to Ibrahim Nathoo, one of the most senior community members, who lived in Nairobi. I watched as the Aga Khan sat on one side of a giant pair of scales and raw, uncut diamonds were placed on the other side until the scales balanced. The diamonds had been purchased from De Beers of South Africa on the understanding that they would be used for the weighing ceremony and then resold to De Beers for the same purchase price. The deal was negotiated by Count Abdullah Hasham

Gangji of Zanzibar. Money for the purchase of the diamonds was donated by the Ismaili community. People contributed what they could. There were, of course, some rich families who contributed large sums. Among those in Tanganyika were the families of Habib Punja; Hussein Nasser Shariff; Jaffer Haji, who owned a jeweller's shop and also sold ivory and carpets; and, of course, my father. In Zanzibar the wealthy families included those of Count Abdullah Shariff, Count Abdullah Hasham Gangji and Count Jindani. The wealthy Kenyan families included those of Count Fatehali Dhala; Sir Eboo Pirbhai; Ahamad Mahommed; Hasham Jamal; and Suleman Virjee.

The money raised during the Diamond Jubilee provided the core capital to set up institutions such as the Diamond Jubilee Investment Trust, which then provided low-interest loans to enable members of the community to build or purchase their own homes. Thus, there was no question of the money being given for the Aga Khan's personal use. It came back to the Ismailis and was utilized for their social and economic progress.

I remember one day as we were driving through the city, the Aga Khan told me that he was going to advise the women in our community to adopt western clothing. He explained that once the women began wearing European-type clothes, which included the colonial frock, they would have an incentive to improve their health through exercise and better food. And so it happened: The Aga Khan issued a *firman* and over the years the result was as he had predicted. The women began to lose some weight and their health, too, improved immensely.

The Diamond Jubilee was also when the Aga Khan changed my name from Noordin (meaning 'light of religion') to Al Noor ('the light'). He kept referring to Noor around the house and people asked him, 'Who is Noor?' He replied, 'Noordin. His name is Al Noor now.' And the Begum Aga Khan, Mata Salamat, told me, 'Don't forget now, your name is Al Noor.' So I changed my name by deed poll. My second son was born on 9 August, the day before the Diamond Jubilee celebration and the Aga Khan named him Diamond. My third son was born in 1948 and the Aga Khan named him Jemal-ud-din, after the great Afghan leader Jamaldin Alafghan.

Later, I accompanied the Aga Khan to Madagascar as his aide-de-camp in an entourage that included Sir Eboo Pirbhai, Abdullah Hasham Gangji, Fatehali Dhala and Ibrahim Nathoo, as well as a member of the Javeri family from Bombay. I was the only young man to be included in that august company.

The year 1946 was also the beginning of my involvement in the community's educational affairs: I was appointed Honorary Joint Secretary of the Ismailia Education Committee. At that time the Chairman of the H.H. Aga Khan Provincial Education Board was Jafferali Ali Meghji.

* * * *

In the following years I became quite popular in political and business circles, and was invited to Government House and parties. I was often asked to give speeches to organizations like the Rotary club as well as within the Ismaili community. Life was very enjoyable. I played tennis and I danced. I am very fond of dancing – ballroom as well as Indian folk dances, and I went to music parties regularly. Although I was brought up in a staunchly religious family and went to mosque and offered prayers regularly, because of my absence from home my knowledge of my religion was somewhat limited. I accepted my Ismaili faith but did not yet understand its intellectual and spiritual dimensions. Later, when I went to England, I read the late Aga Khan's Memoirs and that was the beginning of my knowledge of the Ismaili faith.

The next watershed in my life came in 1950, when the British Governor, Sir Edward Twining, suggested to me that I would make better use of my capacities by going back to England to study law. However, my father did not like the idea. He could see no reason for my abandoning a business in which I was doing so well, to go and study abroad. He also thought that, as a married man, I had an obligation to continue earning an income to maintain my family. Besides, my brother was not interested in the shop and my father had hoped that I would continue the business tradition he had started. He warned me that if I decided to go, he would not pay the costs. After several acrimonious discussions, I told him that I intended to consult the late Aga Khan for his advice. I therefore wrote to His Highness, explaining my situation, and I received a reply in a letter dated 13 September 1950. He wrote:

I have carefully thought over your letter about your proposal to go and study for the Bar and to take up a political and public career later.

We very badly need men like you in public life. I have been
worrying that my [spiritual] children out there have not got the
proper kind of spokesmen in sufficiently large numbers to help
in the stormy times that will come in the next few years and that
will be of long duration. For these reasons I cannot but feel that
it is a blessing that you should have had these ideas.

On the other hand, he pointed out that my personal life and future
financial security should also be taken into consideration in making
the decision.

With this encouragement, I reviewed my financial situation. I had
saved money that I had earned in the business and also had shares in
various enterprises. My wife thought it would be a good career move
and that I had the brains and the capacity to do it. Her father, Count
V.M. Nazerally, also thought it would be a good idea. In 1951 I told
my father that I was going. Looking back, I think that had it not been
for the Aga Khan's reply, I would not have had the courage to do so.
As a result of this advice, my father reluctantly accepted my decision.

So, I flew to England with my wife and three children to start a
new phase in my life.

* * * *

In London, we lived in a house on Preston Road, near the
underground station of that name on the way to Harrow. It was
inexpensive but large enough to accommodate the five of us. Once
we had settled in, I went to the central offices of the Inns of Court,
at Lincoln's Inn Fields. The man in charge was friendly and I
explained to him that I had not sat for the matriculation exams
because of the Second World War, but that my teachers and
headmaster had been confident that I would have passed. After
chatting with me about my business and background in properties he
suggested that I apply to Lincoln's Inn, which specialized in
conveyancing while the other Inns were more oriented towards
common law, which meant practising mostly in court. He also gave
me a letter of recommendation. I applied and was accepted by
Lincoln's Inn.

At Lincoln's Inn, unlike in other universities and colleges, students
did not mix much, except at formal dinners. They attended lectures
and then went home. However, once again, I found myself popular

and was soon elected Vice-Chairman of the Inns of Court Students' Union without having canvassed for the position.

In 1951 the late Aga Khan appointed me President of the Ismailia Council in the UK. Initially, the Ismaili residents of the city had no *jamatkhana* (centre for congregation) and the well-known Indian Javeri family made their house available for prayers. On the instructions of the Aga Khan, I negotiated the purchase of a building, 51 Kensington Court, London, which became a centre for the Ismaili community in England. It housed a prayer hall as well as the Ismailia Social and Residential Club.

The building was opened on behalf of the Aga Khan by the Begum Aga Khan, Mata Salamat, on 17 May 1953. She read out a message from the Aga Khan, in which he said, 'Although very few of you are residents in Great Britain, the moment you are in this country you belong to the fraternity which is known as the Jamat of England; and the Headquarters of this fraternity are now in London.' In his message the Aga Khan added that the Centre would be 'a social and religious centre as well as educational in the highest sense of the word' for Ismailis 'who, for better instruction, for commerce or for pleasure come to this greatest of all cities'. Urging the community to 'build up a library of Ismaili literature and Islamic studies in History and Cultural and Political Thought of the past,' The Aga Khan added, 'Everyone of you must consider this as a home from home in the true sense of the word; that is, where your spirit gets rest from the wear and tear of life.'

In addition to my responsibilities for Ismaili community affairs in the United Kingdom, I became very involved in the activities at East Africa House, situated at Marble Arch. I used to go there regularly and met many people; and that is where, as stated earlier, I met Mwalimu Nyerere. I did not see him again until 1955, when the British Council in Dar es Salaam asked me to become a member of a committee which evaluated scholarship applications. He, too, was on that committee.

We stayed in London until 1954. Shirin, the boys and I travelled together to France, where we called on the late Aga Khan and were invited to dinner at his residence, Yakimour. At the dinner, Prince Aly Khan invited us to have lunch with him at his home, so the next day we went to the beautiful Chateau de l'Horizon. I then saw Shirin and the children off on a ship from Marseilles and went back to London.

His Highness Aga Khan III, Sultan Muhammad Shah, signs documents for the purchase of the building in London that became the centre of the Ismaili community in the United Kingdom.

The Begum Aga Khan, Mata Salamat, opens the Ismaili community centre in London.

In January 1954 I started preparing for my final Bar examinations, which were to be in the middle of the year. Three months before the exams, my closest friend, Amir Karimjee, a member of the well-known Karimjee Jivanjee family, who was always on the go and very sporting, told me, 'Why don't you take a break and come with me to the Continent? We'll go and visit my family there.' So he bought a new sports car and we drove through the Continent to Switzerland. After three weeks I went back to London and he continued on to Spain.

I sat my examinations but returned home before the results came out. Later, I was in Tanga on the way to Nairobi when I received a telegram reading 'Our Nick has done the trick', informing me that I had passed my Bar exams. I went to London to be called to the Bar at Lincoln's Inn and was admitted to the Advocates' Roll in Dar es Salaam in 1954.

I started working with Dharsee and McRoberts. McRoberts had been a High Court judge. Dharsee was a good conveyancing lawyer and an excellent writer but not very active in court. Born in a Zanzibar family, he had been educated at Oxford University. Later, when I started private practice, I established the offices of Al Noor Kassum and Company Advocates on the first floor of a new building, Avalon House, built by my father next to the Avalon Cinema. Dharsee and McRoberts also moved their offices there.

Tom Tyrell, the Mayor of Dar es Salaam, asked me if I would like to be retained as a lawyer for the First Permanent Building Society – and, of course, I accepted with pleasure. My practice consisted mostly of conveyancing, with the occasional criminal case. One of my clients was Abbas Sykes, a founder member of the first African political party in Tanganyika – the Tanganyika African National Union (TANU). He was charged with reckless driving and I managed to get him acquitted. I used to visit my father-in-law on his sisal estate in the Moshi area regularly, and during one visit the Mwangi Mkuu – leader – of the Chaggaa Council, Thomas Marealle, approached me. He said that their lawyer, Tiger Thomas, who was from Bermuda, had left and he asked me to represent the Wachaggaa in legal matters.

I earned a good income from my practice, enough to pay off my debts and educate my sons in the UK. I shared my wealth with my family members – whenever one of them had difficulties, I sent them some funds. As the number of clients increased, I employed an elderly lawyer to help run the practice. When the First Permanent Building Society put up their building on the main road in Dar es Salaam, I moved my offices there. Over time, my father reconciled himself to the fact that I would not be helping him to run the family business; nonetheless, he was pleased with my success..

In 1954 the late Aga Khan appointed me Administrator of the Aga Khan schools in Tanganyika, which meant automatic membership of the Indian Education Authority. The Aga Khan also bestowed the title of 'Varas' on me – at the age of 30 years, I was the youngest Ismaili to be given that title. I moved the office of the Administrator to the building owned by the First Permanent Building Society. I was helped in my work as Education Administrator by an Executive Officer, S.V. Peerwani. Rather old-fashioned, he came from India but was a very methodical man, excellent at his work. We got on marvellously. During my ten-year tenure as Administrator, the Ismaili community built many schools and the current Aga Khan made available a large number of scholarships for students to go abroad for higher education.

Ismaili schools had been in existence in what is now Tanzania since 1905, when the Shia Imami Ismaili Kanyashala opened its doors in Zanzibar. It was a school for girls and by 1914 it had 179 pupils ranging in age from 5 years to 15 years. The building was renovated in 1931 and is now the government-run Hurumzi Primary School. In 1907, the Ismaili community in Zanzibar founded the Ismailia Aga Khan School for boys. By 1913, it had 176 pupils. The school building is now the Institute of Kiswahili Research. Bagamoyo, in what is now mainland Tanzania, was also the site of an Aga Khan school in the early 1900s. The school is now the Mwanamakuka Primary School.

The schools built by the Ismaili community were among those with the best educational standards in the country and their intake began to be multiracial as independence approached and the colonial rules enforcing segregated education were relaxed. The racial integration of the student intake continued after independence. One of the Ismaili schools, Mzizima High School, was particularly known for the quality of its science and maths teaching. Tambaza – now known as the Tambaza Aga Khan School – was also very good; some of its students later went on to study at Harvard and Yale universities in the USA. The Aga Khan provided scholarships for hundreds of students to go abroad for university studies during my period as

Education Administrator. They were mostly for subjects such as economics and engineering, which would be of immediate practical use to the country.

For example, in 1959 there were 86 students in the final year of secondary education in Ismaili schools. In addition, 57 had got through their secondary education and were preparing to go on to higher school education or other studies. Of this total of 143 students (72 boys and 71 girls), 56 wanted to have a career as teachers, six wanted to go into the nursing profession, 27 wanted to be engineers, 11 preferred chartered accountancy, four intended to become architects, five wanted to go into medicine, one wanted to be a pharmacist, one wanted to take up law, one wanted to be a journalist, 16 intended to go on to university, two were interested in radiography, two wanted to make their careers in business administration, eight had various other professions in mind, and three had not yet decided on their future career. It was obvious that they and their parents had taken to heart the Aga Khan's frequent advice to stop thinking in terms of being little *dukawallahs* (shopkeepers).

Under British rule, Asians, like the other communities, paid a special tax through which schools were partly funded. Two-thirds of the construction costs came from that fund and one-third was provided by the community that was building the schools. The architect of the Ismaili schools built during my tenure was Rhemtulla Kaderali, who had recently migrated to Tanganyika from India. As the political situation began to change, even before independence, on the instructions of His Highness Prince Karim Al Husseini, the Aga Khan, who succeeded his grandfather as Imam of the Ismaili Muslims in 1957, I opened the Ismaili schools to all races as soon as it became possible to do so.

It was a very busy period for me. In addition to my governmental responsibilities and work as the Education Administrator of the Ismaili community in Tanganyika, I was given other assignments by the Aga Khan. For instance, in 1962 the Aga Khan asked Jimmy Verjee, a lawyer from Nairobi who was the Aga Khan Education Administrator in Kenya, Zaher Ahmed, who was attached to In-dustrial Promotion Services (IPS) and myself to assist in drafting a new constitution for the Ismaili community in Africa, to replace the one issued in the 1920s. Jimmy Verjee and I spent two weeks in Gstaad, Switzerland, working all day on the basis of the Aga Khan's directives and then presenting our output to the Aga Khan every evening for his comments. He would call us in at half past five every morning to discuss the previous day's output and then we would start that day's work. In 1962, the Aga Khan called a conference in Kenya to discuss the proposed new constitution. The participants included Jimmy Verjee, Zaher Ahmed, the President of the Ismailia Supreme Council, community presidents at the national level, presidents of the Ismaili Associations, myself, and various other people.

In 1956, the Asians in Tanganyika formed the Asian Association (which I decided not to join), a political organization led by, among others, Mohamed Ratansi and Amir Habib Jamal. Amir was an intellectual with a degree from a university in Calcutta and he assisted Mwalimu Julius Nyerere considerably. When I joined Mwalimu's cabinet later, we were colleagues. It so happened that we became neighbours and my wife Yasmin and I used to play bridge regularly with him and his wife Shasu.

* * * *

In October 1958, I was appointed to replace G.N. Houri, a Greek lawyer, as Temporary Nominated Member of the Tanganyika Legislative Council while he was absent from the Territory. At that time the Legislative Council included 15 African, Asian and European elected representatives, each race having elected one representative from each of the five provinces. The following year they were to elect five more representatives each from the remaining five provinces. There was also one Arab representative in the Legislative Council.

Thus I participated, on 14 October 1958, in the thirty-fourth session of the Legislative Council, sitting on the Government bench. The Governor, Sir Richard Turnbull, addressed the Members. His speech highlighted the concerns of the British government at a time when Tanganyika was steadily moving towards self-government. He noted that the session was an important one in the history of Tanganyika because it was the first in which elected Members were taking part.

Sir Richard then turned his attention to 'certain misapprehensions which seem to have arisen concerning what is commonly referred to as Government's policy of multi-racialism'. He noted:

A belief appears to exist amongst some people that a 'multi-racial' – or, as I would prefer to call it, and intend to call it, a 'non-racial' – policy will, in some way or other prevent the Africans of Tanganyika from reaching their full political stature and from playing their proper part in the government of this country.

The Governor denied that would be so. He recalled that the UK Minister of State for Foreign Affairs had informed the UN General Assembly in February 1957 that the participation of Africans in both legislative and executive branches of the government was bound to increase as the educational, social and economic progress of the African community in Tanganyika continued:

> In terms of population the Africans are and always will be an overwhelming majority in Tanganyika and, as the country progresses, it is right and proper, as indeed it is natural and inevitable, that African participation both in the legislature and in the executive should steadily increase. It is not intended, and never has been intended, that parity should be a permanent feature of the Tanganyika scene.

Sir Richard added:

> On the other hand it is intended, and always has been intended, that the fact that when self-government is eventually attained both the legislature and the government are likely to be predominantly African should in no way affect the security of the rights and interests of those minority communities who have made their homes in Tanganyika.

He said that he attached 'the greatest importance' to maintaining and fostering the 'Tanganyikan outlook' of the Civil Service,

> and, as a corollary, to the training of local people to occupy senior posts not only in the Civil Service but also in commerce and in industry […] I intend to pursue this policy as rapidly as our educational and training resources allow […] there are no limits to the fields which can be entered, or to the level which can be reached in the Civil Service by local candidates who have

the necessary qualifications, the strength of character and the personal aptitude – and above all that scrupulous trustworthiness that must be the hall-mark of the Civil Servant.

Turning to the different forms of local government in the rural areas, the Governor once again stressed the need to respect minority rights and interests. He said 'an essential pre-requisite' to the formation of District Councils had been 'acceptance of the principle that membership was not necessarily confined to members of any one race; and that any resident of the area, whatever the community to which he belonged, would be eligible to serve on such a council'. This did not mean a prohibition of purely African District Councils 'in districts in which non-African interests are so limited that the setting up of a purely African District Council would not be inconsistent with accepted local government principles,' but,

> in areas where non-African interests are substantial, the proper and orderly development of local government would be stultified by the exclusion of non-African representation; in such districts any alternative to District Councils would involve an undesirable diminution in the range of local government responsibility or some redistribution of responsibility which would inevitably be wasteful of men and money.'

In addition, the Governor addressed various other issues, including government proposals for 'the transition of native customary tenure into individual ownership' and urged the Legislative Council Members to 'bear in mind the far-reaching influence which their decisions will have on the social and economic development of the territory' when voting on the proposals. He also told the Legislative Council Members that they would soon be discussing a Bill to give legislative authority to agreements between the government and De Beers Consolidated Mines Limited for equal partnership in Williamson Diamonds Limited at Mwadui in Tanganyika. As I read through the Bill later, I did not know that it would be the precursor to another development in my life: in 1970 Mwalimu Nyerere appointed me Deputy General Manager of Williamson Diamonds Limited.

Replying to Sir Richard's speech, Chief John Maruma, a Nominated Member, observed that it was the first time a governor had ever addressed the Legislative Council. He supported all the major points made by the Governor, describing the address as 'an inspiring and constructive speech' and 'a genuine, sincere, forthright and serious appreciation of the problems facing our beloved country'.

Mwalimu Julius Nyerere, one of the three Members representing Eastern Province, noted that 'during the short period that His Excellency has been in this country he has earned the respect of all sections of the community'. He took issue with the idea that Tanganyika required a special multiracial policy:

Countries in other parts of the world are multi-racial; Great Britain is multi-racial in population; India is multi-racial in population. There is not one country in the world which is not multi-racial in population. We do not hear talk of multi-racial policy in Britain. We do not hear talk of multi-racial policy in the United States or other countries in the world which are necessarily multi-racial in population.

Mwalimu said it was the highlighting of a multiracial policy for Tanganyika which had created misapprehension.

When there was an emphasis in this country on multi-racial policies we felt, and with great justification, that there was something sinister about this multi-racial policy in Tanganyika. We expected that we would get some clear definition of this which would make it clear why, when we know all over the world people of different races live together, why here in Tanganyika we should have this emphasis of race – whether before that 'race' we place 'multi' or 'non'. It is for that reason, Sir, that with great respect, I do not even like the word 'non-racial' to be used in any policy in Tanganyika. What is 'non-racial'? If you start, Sir, with 'multi-racial' and you start with 'multi' in big capital letters, you are bound to end up with 'multi' in some small letters and 'racial' in big letters. If you start with 'non', even in big capitals, by the time you end, Sir, 'non' is not there at all, and you have 'racial' in big letters. I feel we should have nothing to do with any kind of racial policies in this country.' He told the Members, 'What we want in this country is that every citizen of Tanganyika, irrespective of his race, as long as he owes allegiance to Tanganyika, is a complete and equal citizen with anyone else.

Mwalimu also welcomed the Governor's assurance that purely African District Councils could be formed in areas where the numbers or interests of non-Africans did not justify the necessity of having them on District Councils. He said the government's emphasis till then on the racial composition of District Councils had made them unpopular and 'led in some areas to very unfortunate results'.

On the proposed transformation of communal land tenure into private ownership, Mwalimu acknowledged that 'it is very difficult to develop the land under the present system of tenure,' but said it also had many advantages. He cautioned that the process of change should be carried out slowly and carefully because it had been the only form of land tenure in Tanganyika over the generations. In addition,

> other countries which have attempted to introduce or have introduced a purely individual tenure have lost the advantages of land remaining in the hands of the country generally, and I know that many countries are regretting the fact that the whole community has lost control of the land. Some are making attempts to revert to the position which they lost when the country belonged to the community generally. Therefore, to change from a system, whether you call it tribal or not, where land does belong to the community to a system where a piece of land belongs to an individual, in the sense in which my jacket belongs to me, is a very revolutionary change and the only thing I suggest to Government is that we go very slowly, that we take a long time to consider this. There is nothing we can lose in taking a long time explaining it to the people.

He said his own personal view was that

> some form of individual guarantee of security to a person is necessary, a revolutionary change which would make it possible for a community which hitherto has never said 'this piece of land is mine' in the sense in which a piece of bread is mine [to do so].'

However, he urged the government to 'consider whether there are not other means of securing the same effect without in effect giving land to individuals. We do not want, Sir, to make a revolutionary change today and then, 20, 40, 50, 60 years from now find that we have committed a great mistake and that we have to revert again to the old system.' In view of this statement, his policies after independence were not surprising.

Among the speakers that day was Mrs. Sofia Mustafa (Northern Province), who described the proposed increase in education facilities for Africans, announced by the Governor, as 'a wise move'. She said that in Asian schools, too, 'the standard leaves very much to be desired' and some parents were therefore sending their children abroad to study. In contrast, the standard of education in European schools was much higher. Declaring herself to be 'one of those people who, like George Orwell, believe that all men are equal but some are more equal than others', she said that such inequality, however, should not be based on race.

I feel that it is worth serious consideration that this comparatively better type of education which exists in European schools in the Territory be made open for children of other races gradually and by stages. It does seem fair that those who require it and demand it, of whatever race they may be, may have the opportunity of taking advantage of the best possible education offered in the Territory and not be deprived of it only because of their race.

The next day, after a number of other Legislative Council Members had spoken, I was given the opportunity to make my maiden speech. It is reproduced in full here for a reason that will soon become apparent.

Mr. Speaker, Sir, I am a new and young Member of this Honourable House, and consider myself comparatively a novice, but I wish in my own little way to say what I can to welcome the address which His Excellency the Governor presented here yesterday. In the first place, and in conjunction with other members of this Honourable House, I would like to welcome His Excellency the Governor and Lady Turnbull to Tanganyika.

Rather than deviate from the subject, I will concentrate on a few points that have been made by His Excellency in his address.

In the first place a most important constitutional development was announced, and I think very little has been said about it. It is in the second paragraph of that address, when he says that the next step which this country shall take will be towards responsible government.

His Excellency then, in his following paragraph, says that for that purpose a post-elections committee will be appointed to discuss the terms of reference. Am I not correct in assuming, or am I wrong in saying, that one is a concommitant of the other, and that the attainment of responsible government shall necessarily be one of the terms of reference? If that is the case, then we shall have moved towards making a progressive step towards getting self-government for this country, and 'self-determination' is a word which I would prefer to use, because I think it is the people of Tanganyika who must make their choice.

In case I should be accused of repetition, I would like to endorse a statement which was made a little earlier, in the first speech, in fact, by the Honourable Mr. Nyerere, in connection with this naming of the policy of being 'multi-racial' or 'non-racial'. 'Multi-racial' has its stigma. It means representation of the various races. 'Non-racial', on the other hand, is a negative statement. It is an epithet which says in the negation that there shall be no particular race which shall control the future policy of this country. If that is the case, should we use the word 'racial' at all? Should we not say – and I would like to use here the word which was used by an earlier speaker, and that was the Honourable Mr. [A.] Roden [Southern Province] and that has a ring to it which appeals to me – the 'oneness' of things? Should it not be a oneness of Tanganyika nationhood? Would that not be the conception that we are trying to seek? It would equally, I say, Sir, be correct in saying that to attach the name of 'European', 'African' or 'Asian' to any Government body is today an anachronism.

I talk, for instance, in terms of the European Education Authority, or the Indian Education Authority or the African Advisory Committee. If we are going to consider speaking in terms of one nationhood and a non-racial policy, which the oneness implies, then surely we should begin immediately by implementing that in some constructive and concrete form, and I would say, Sir, that an authority of oneness be immediately implemented and an education system on that basis be introduced in this country.

I shall have a few more things to say about education a little later when I get to that part of His Excellency's address, Sir.

I then focused on my vision of the future Tanganyika, keeping in mind that its population already consisted of several races and that in a democracy voters should have the right to make their own choices:

'In talking about 'non-racialism', 'multi-racialism', 'common policy', a 'oneness of things', I go to another statement. I am afraid I am cribbing, perhaps, for somebody spoke a little earlier and I was forestalled. It is in connection with the statement that the future Government of this country should be predominantly African. That is, of course, from a practical point of view quite correct, but I go a little further in saying that the future Government of this country shall not be predominantly African. It shall be predominantly of the people chosen by this country, may the chosen one be an African, an Asian, a European, a Chinese, or anyone.

We have had this oneness question put to us and I am sure for practical purposes that there will be a predominantly African government, but hypothetically there is a possibility, if the right man arose in this country and said 'I shall lead you on the right path and I shall give you what you want', there would not be one soul from the nine million people of this country who will say 'Nay, we shall not choose him'. If he is the right man he will go where he deserves to go.

I now go to my pet subject – education. The Honourable Mrs. Mustafa very rightly said that the standard of education being imparted at Asian schools was comparatively low in the Northern Province. I go a little further, and say that the standard of education throughout the Territory is not as one would like it. That probably applies to African education, and perhaps not to European education, but I say, 'Where is the problem?' The problem lies in the fact that we have three systems of education. The problem lies in the fact that our teachers are being separated in those three systems. The problem lies in the fact that we do not have a common policy as far as the education of our children is concerned.

It is not easy for any Government, and I say that with due deference, to make a statement and say: 'We shall tomorrow have 150 secondary schools' because that is financially impossible. But if we have a principle, and that principle says that we shall be one, then at the risk of finance, I say: 'Let us be one, even if the education imparted be slightly lower'. I say: 'Let us get together and think on that basis'. I do not think for one instant there would be any difficulty in at least saying straight away that our secondary education schools should be all together. We have a half dozen secondary schools being built at the moment by the Indian Education Authority. We have a first-class secondary school – public school is probably the better word for it – being built at Iringa. We have 24 secondary schools under the auspices of the African Advisory Committee, and of these, four are going to produce Higher School Certificate children, and in the Indian Education Authority I believe there is one at the moment, and a second one contemplated.

Sir, suppose we were to pool those resources and we made secondary education in any of these schools available to a person of ability, irrespective of his race, caste or creed or colour. If the child at his Standard VIII level or Common Entrance, or whatever you like to call it, were to have the necessary ability to go forward in that particular type of education, then he must not be denied that opportunity. He must be given the full forces of the country behind him to say: 'You are the person who will in future be our economist, and we will see you will get the sort of education which will make an economist out of you,' and it shall not be the privilege of the few.

However, being a member of the legal profession, we always say there is the alternative, and the alternative I am saying at the moment is this. We are seeking teachers in our various schools. We are seeking teachers of any race, and I know of one organisation which is looking for African-trained teachers to fill its establishment. Makerere [University in Kampala] is at the moment producing sufficient numbers of trained teachers to fill the requirements of Government schools. Cannot that stream be enlarged, Sir? Can we not find a few more teachers brought through that wonderful institution? It is a monopoly of Uganda, unfortunately. I wish it had been in Tanganyika. However, that is perhaps a thing to come. Can we not make full use of those teachers and get the teachers irrespective of what school they may go to? Cannot something be done on those lines ?

The Honourable Mr. [D.N.M.] Bryceson [Northern Province] spoke of the question of the University College and as to where it was going to be placed. I am sorry to say that I loathe to think in terms of any place which is within a few miles of the border of Kenya because I say that place is influenced very easily by what Kenya is doing today or tomorrow.

The monopoly of education systems today is in Nairobi, and if my learned friend, the Honourable Mr. Bryceson has a sufficient number of children who seek teacher training, they may go next door. Shall we not have this teachers' training institute, or the University College, more centralised? Shall we not have it somewhere near the doors of Dar es Salaam? Shall we not give Dar es Salaam, which has been denied any first-class educational institution, its rightful place as the capital of this country and say: 'No, you shall have a certain amount of say and influence on this University College? But I do not want to seem parochial about this. I do not say it should be in Dar es Salaam. I say it should be on the Ulugurus. I say we should have it somewhere high up on those beautiful mountains near Morogoro, where the air and the climate is conducive to hard work. Mountains where there are no distractions of city life, mountains where our children who will be studying there will have the opportunity of vigorous physical exercise. Let us make them do some mountaineering as well.

And then I am led from talking of Morogoro to discuss the question which I think is the last item that I shall touch upon, and that is the question of communications: In that respect I say Morogoro is the potential Clapham Junction of Tanganyika. It can in the future be the meeting link for the rest of the Territory. It should develop on those lines. From Dar es Salaam you go up to Morogoro and from Morogoro you can go north, south, or west. I hope not too many will go west!

Therefore, are we not going to consider developing communications from Morogoro? The Northern Province and the Tanga Province – Tanga at the moment buys all its produce and all its requirements from Mombasa. Arusha and Moshi buy all their requirements from Nairobi, or from Mombasa, because they have a direct link. But Dar es Salaam, which is our main port, bringing in produce, is left on its own. Can we not say that we shall help Dar es Salaam find its rightful place in Tanganyika as the capital if that be so? Shall we not say: 'We shall help it find its communication'? The new Mikumi line will certainly go towards [Marian] Lady Chesham [Southern Highlands Province, who had earlier welcomed the positive economic effects the railway line would have for farmers in her province], and I hope one day Lady Chesham will have the pleasure of seeing that line so that she is able either through those first-class roads or communications to say 'I am closer to Dar es Salaam than I ever was before', and the same might be said about Arusha or Moshi.

I know the answer is 'We have no money', but we have not got any money. We have never been a rich country and we don't pretend to be a rich country at the moment, but we must have the hope and the faith in the potential value of the country and to think that we shall overcome our difficulties, and unless you begin with that premise, the cause will be lost, and if I were to say 'Let us have that road and have these communications within a period of years' I should be talking something which is quite ridiculous and impracticable. I say, 'Let us have a policy'. I say 'Let us have a policy of a five-year programme, a ten-year programme, a 20-year programme, and as time and opportunities arise, implement that programme accordingly, but make that programme now so that we know what the next step is, and what goal we have to reach, and towards that goal we should work. We shall say: 'Now what shall we do?', and think of Mikumi.

I think, of course, from Kilosa's and from Kimamba's point of view it is a very good thing for the Territory that this line has been put in, and I wholeheartedly supported that Motion [to approve construction of the line], not because I was on this side of the House, but because I believed it was the right thing.

The railways would probably say: 'Oh, if we have these communications brought in. the railways will suffer', but I say,

Sir, and most humbly and respectfully, that that is a false statement in that it is a false approach to economy. Is the greater benefit of the Territory which it may derive more important, or will the little loss that the railways suffer be more important? You will not be able to balance one budget, but that budget is covered by a greater budget, and it is the greater budget we have got to look at. I say, Sir, on those lines we should have this policy which will think in terms of economic development over a period of years.

I missed one point when I was talking about education, and if I may just make a slight reference to that I should be much obliged. With your permission, Sir, I referred to His Excellency's statement in connection with St. Michael and St. George's School. It was stated when originally the plan was conceived that we shall make places available there for non-European children. I hope, Sir, that takes place very, very soon because I believe that unless we are able to get admission into that school at the outset, later on you may – and I make a statement of apology to the United States of America – be put into the embarrassing position which the Government of the United States has been put into in connection with its policy of Little Rock. Let us avoid that situation a few years – ten years – hence, and let us have our children think from this moment in terms of tolerance and charity – a word which was so ably used by my learned friend Mr. [D.P.] Kidaha Makwaia [Assistant Minister, Lands].

My speech had an unexpected consequence. At the end of the day's sitting, Mwalimu Nyerere ran across the Chamber to me and said, 'What on earth are you doing on that side of the House? You should join us and run for one of the Asian seats in next year's elections.' I told him I had never thought of standing in the elections and he said, 'I would like you to.'

However, later, when the leaders of the Asian Association were told of his proposal, they objected to my invited to become a politician. Labelling me a capitalist, they said I had no interest in political activity and, since I was not a member of the Association, should not be given TANU's support. Mwalimu called me to a meeting at which these objections were made. I took a sheet of paper and wrote on it,

I am not a member of the Asian Association. I believe in non-racial secular politics. But I have read the manifesto of the Asian Association which I support, and in addition I shall advocate that the first immediate step should be the establishment of a responsible government, and I shall, through the concept of a Tanganyika nationhood made up of all the people who live here, work for self-government.

I then expounded on my beliefs with regard to the future and passed the note to Mwalimu. He read it and said, 'This is good enough for me. You believe in everything we are doing. You are not a member of either of our parties, but you say that you are prepared to follow our principles.' He then asked me if I would like to run for the Dodoma seat, with TANU's full support, and I said yes.

So I stood for elections in Dodoma, alongside the African candidate, Malim Malum Kihere, who was from Tanga, and the European candidate, a Dr Hana, who was from one of the Christian missions. An Asian lawyer named Keeka stood against me. Bibi Titi Mohammad was chosen by TANU to speak at my rallies on the party's behalf. As I did not speak Kiswahili fluently, I delivered my speeches in English and they were translated sentence by sentence. Despite this, the support from TANU did the trick and I won hands down. Dodoma is situated in the Central Province, a region inhabited by the Gogo tribe, and in the Legislative Council I used to joke that the three elected Members were the first Gogos to be elected to the Council. It was only in the next elections that the Gogo elected representatives from within their own community.

Mwalimu persuaded TANU to change its rule limiting membership to Africans, and from 1959 to 1964 I was the Chief Whip of the TANU parliamentary party. In the lead-up to independence, Mwalimu Nyerere made it clear in his speeches that he was against the adoption of any 'isms' – be they racism, tribalism or any ideological 'ism'. He said everyone should be judged on their own merits and the people of Tanganyika should have the freedom to elect any citizen of the country to parliament, irrespective of race, religion or any other such identity factors. At no time did he threaten violence if we were not given independence soon. I think the word 'violence' did not exist in his political dictionary until 1978, when Ugandan President Idi Amin's troops invaded our country and I saw him for the first time become really angry and prepared to use force to defend the territorial integrity of his nation.

In my speeches, I talked about how badly non-whites had been treated under British rule, for example by not being allowed to attend schools and hospitals on an equal basis. I said that what we were struggling for was not a reversal of the situation, not for the opportunity to discriminate against whites but rather to establish a society in which everyone would be equal. In other words, what we were working towards was a meritocratic society. I was in favour of a society based on social welfare, but, like Mwalimu Nyerere, I opposed extremism in either direction. Mwalimu and I used to meet frequently and he sometimes came to my home, and the discussions with him crystallized my views further.

In 1961, a Constitutional Conference was held in Dar es Salaam, to which I was invited, to discuss the final steps to independence. The Colonial Secretary, Ian McLeod, flew in from Britain for the conference. Finally, on 9 December 1961, Tanganyika became an independent nation.

3

WINDS OF CHANGE IN AFRICA

The 'wind of change', as British Prime Minister Harold Macmillan famously termed it, was already sweeping across Africa. In 1957, Ghana had become the first sub-Saharan African country to win independence from a colonial power. Guinea had followed the next year and then had come a steady stream of decolonization. In 1960, west and central Africa had seen the birth of the following independent countries: Senegal, Central African Republic, Mauritania, Gabon, Benin, Chad, Niger, Nigeria, the Congo (later known as Zaire and now the Democratic Republic of Congo), Congo (Brazaville), Côte d'Ivoire, Burkina Faso, Togo, and Mali. Madagascar, off the eastern coast of the continent, had also become independent. Now it was the turn of Tanganyika.

Even at that time, Mwalimu Nyerere was thinking of East Africans uniting to benefit the people of the region. As independence neared, he declared that if Kenya and Uganda were granted independence soon and were willing to join Tanganyika in a federation, Tanganyikans would be prepared to delay their independence. However, there was no positive response to this and Tanganyika became independent before Uganda and Kenya. Perhaps if the three countries had united they would have become a continental economic powerhouse, and Africa as a whole would have benefited from their example. Mainland Tanzania is the only part of Africa that has never experienced a political assassination, and that, too, would have been a useful example for the rest of Africa.

Independence Day was full of promise. Dar es Salaam was bright with colours: shops and streets were hung with multicoloured bunting and the new green-yellow-black Tanganyika flag; all the residents of the city were dressed in their best clothes. Everyone in the streets was smiling and full of goodwill. Precisely at midnight, a team of Tanganyikans had lighted the freedom beacon on top of Mount Kilimanjaro, and the flames could be seen even across the border in Kenya. It was a signal of our determination to create a society in which social and economic justice would prevail. Mwalimu Nyerere became the first Prime Minister and then resigned soon thereafter, and Rashidi Kawawa became Prime Minister. Then, on 9 December 1962, when the country became a republic, Mwalimu became President and Rashidi Kawawa remained Prime Minister. I was extremely elated by all these events, in fact almost euphoric, because, as a member of the legislature, I felt I had made a personal, even if modest, contribution to the movement towards independence.

Earlier, in May 1961, after Tanganyika had been granted internal self-government, I had been appointed Parliamentary Secretary, Ministry of Education and Information. My Minister was Oscar Kambona. On 9 December he was appointed Minister of Foreign Affairs and replaced by Solomon Eliufoo. At that time, only 480 Tanganyikan Africans had completed secondary school, and fewer than 100 were university graduates. Therefore, our immediate focus was twofold: adult literacy and establishing a university.

Education had been an important issue for me from my earliest days in politics. As shown earlier in these memoirs, my first speech to the colonial Legislative Council had focused on it. Therefore, I was extremely enthusiastic about my new responsibilities. Thanks to generous assistance from Unesco, we managed to raise adult literacy to a point where it was at one time the highest among developing countries. As far as a university was concerned, the University of Dar es Salaam was first established in 1961 as a college of the University of London, then became a constituent college of the University of East Africa and finally a national university in 1970. While construction of a campus began in 1961, TANU gave up its headquarters to the university. It became the site of the university's law school, the first law school in East Africa. Because of His Highness the Aga Khan's commitment to help Tanzania whenever possible, he donated four lecture halls constructed in the same style and to the same standard as lecture halls at Harvard University in the USA; an Olympic-size swimming pool; and a mosque designed by the internationally renowned German architect Walter Gropius, one of the pioneers of the global modern style of architecture. However, as the number of Muslim students increased, the expansion of the mosque led to its losing some of the unique characteristics of Gropius architecture.

We instituted a policy of introducing Kiswahili into the school system with the intention of eventually making the main language of instruction. With the passage of time, Kiswahili took its proper place in the education system while taking into account the fact that English was an essential component internationally from both cultural and educational points of view. Primary school was reduced from eight years to seven. Then, for those who passed, came four years of secondary school (for O-level exams), followed by two more years of higher school education (for A-level exams) before going on to university.

In 1962 I visited Israel together with the Education Minister, Solomon Eliufoo, and found their kibutz system particularly interesting. The overall impression I received was that the Israelis were very determined people. I also travelled to France with the Minister to attend the Unesco General Conference. The Minister fell ill and had to return to Dar es Salaam, so I became head of the Tanganyika delegation. The General Conference had two commissions, the Administrative Commission and the Financial Commission, and I was chosen as rapporteur of the Administrative Commission in 1962.

In 1964, at the next Unesco General Conference, I was Vice-Chairman of the Administrative Commission when the Chairman fell ill. Therefore, I chaired the Administrative Commission that year. On the agenda was the threat posed to the Nubian monuments in Egypt by the proposed construction of the Aswan Dam, whose reservoir would flood the wonders of that ancient civilization. In 1961 Unesco had appointed Prince Sadruddin Aga Khan (the second son of the late Aga Khan, who later became the UN High Commissioner for Refugees) Executive Secretary of its International Action Committee for the Preservation of Nubia. In spite of the Cold War, this committee had brought together prominent archaeologists from Eastern Europe and the West to save the ancient treasures of Abu Simbel, the temples of Philae and Kalabsha and the Christian churches of Nubia. The archaeologists had recommended that the historical monuments facing inundation should be moved to a higher location. The matter was debated in the Administrative Commission and I then presented the case to the Financial Commission, which approved the proposal and sent it on to the

General Conference. The monuments were saved by dismantling the temples stone by stone and then reconstructing them at a higher level.

In August 1962, at the request of Mwalimu Nyerere, I drew up the Memorandum and Articles of Association of Mwananchi Development Corporation Limited. The company was set up to facilitate the economic aspects of TANU's future plans for the country. Thus, its objectives included, *inter alia*, assistance with the settlement of people on land, in villages and in towns; and acquisition of agricultural works, farms, estates, lands, houses and all kinds of movable and immovable property through buying, selling, leasing, hiring, exchanging, or receiving as gifts. Such acquisitions would be for the purpose of founding, establishing and building towns villages, settlements, and suburbs.

The Corporation also intended to

rent, lease, buy and otherwise acquire, build, repair and maintain houses for habitation, shops, stables, barns, store-houses, granaries, water tanks, ponds, wells, mills, offices and all kinds of establishments for work, as well as public institutions such as hospitals, sanatoriums, bathing establishments, schools, workers' homes, theatres and the like.

The Corporation would also

do fishing in rivers, lakes and seas, develop various water industries, exploit the riches of rivers, lakes and seas, carry on shipping, rafting and all kinds of navigation; transport passengers and goods from port to port, load and unload vessels; [and] found subsidiary companies for navigation and fishing. In addition, the Corporation could 'acquire means of transport on land, water and air, and carry on passengers' and goods' transport business, and found subsidiary companies for this purpose.

On the industrial front, its objectives were

to found, develop, manage, extend, establish and acquire workshops and factories in all branches of work and industry; to buy, hire, receive as gift and otherwise acquire all kinds of machinery, implements, tools, materials, plans, inventions, patents or any interests in any patents, which the Company may think suitable for its objects; to let to members of Tanganyika African National Union and others, either as individuals or groups, workshops and factories, machinery and implements, tools and materials on lease, rent or on other conditions; to assist such members in attaining skill, perfection and practice in various branches of work; [and] to found subsidiary companies or co-operative industry.

The Mwananchi Development Corporation intended to

enter into arrangements with governments or other supreme authorities, or municipal authorities, and to procure from such governments or authorities any licences, privileges or concessions, which the Company may think it desirable to obtain, and to carry out, exercise and comply with any such arrangements, licences, privileges and concessions.

To carry out its objectives, the Corporation could

found subsidiary companies with or without share capital, with the view of carrying out all or any of the objects of the Company; establish or assist in the establishment of co-operative labour institutions, societies and groups of all kinds; receive or otherwise acquire and keep shares of any other society, the objects of which are kindred in the whole or in part to the objects of the Company or which carries on any activity which may seem conducive to the benefit of the Company directly or indirectly.

It could also

erect, construct, lay down, enlarge, alter and maintain any roads, railways, tramways, sidings, bridges, reservoirs, shops, stores, factories, buildings, works, plant and machinery necessary or convenient for the Company's business, and contribute to or subsidise the erection, construction and maintenance of any of the above.

An additional objective was 'generally to purchase, take on lease or exchange, hire or otherwise acquire, any real or personal property and any rights or privileges which the Company may think necessary or convenient for the purpose of its business'. Also, the Corporation could

> purchase or otherwise acquire and undertake all or any part of the business, property assets, liabilities and transactions of any person, firm or company carrying on any business which this Company is authorised to carry on [the Articles listed businesses in every sector], or possessed of property suitable for the purpose of the Company.

The subscribers to the Corporation were the Trustees of TANU: Mwalimu Nyerere, Rajabu Salehe Tambwe, Werner Kapinga, Bibi Titi Mohamed, Joseph Kituta Tosiri, Mwali Mwalim Kihere and James Macmillan Simba. The Corporation was incorporated four-and-a-half years before TANU issued the Arusha Declaration expressing determination 'to ensure that the major means of production are under the control and ownership of the Peasants and the Workers themselves through their Government and their Co-operatives' and nationalized banks and several key industries; and nine years and eight months before TANU nationalized all private buildings from which the owners were earning a rent above a certain level. The Mwananchi Development Corporation (MDC) became the economic wing of TANU, for investment and economic empowerment. Its subsidiary companies, such as the Mwananchi Engineering and Construction Company Limited, became well-known names in the construction industry for many years. MDC was later merged with the Tanganyika Development Corporation (successor to the colonial Tanganyika Agricultural Corporation and the Colonial Development Corporation) to create the National Development Corporation, of which I was Chairman of the Board from 1991 to 2002.

Two years after Tanganyika became independent, on 10 December 1963, Zanzibar (including the island of Pemba), off our coast, was also granted independence. The British handed over power to the Arab minority. This soon sparked a revolution led by Sheikh Abeid Karume of the Afro-Shirazi Party and John Okello, a Ugandan soldier. On 12 January 1964 the government was overthrown and

Sultan Sayyid Jamshid ibn Abdullah went into exile. It was logical for Tanganyika and Zanzibar to unite and on 26 April 1964 the two countries formed the United Republic of Tanzania within which Zanzibar still enjoyed some autonomy.

In the new government, I was appointed Parliamentary Secretary, Ministry of Industries, Mineral Resources and Power. There were two Parliamentary Secretaries in the Ministry. My Minister was Abdullah Hanga from Zanzibar. Before the change in portfolio, Mwalimu Nyerere called me in and told me I had a special role to play in the Ministry. 'You are needed there to help look after Hanga,' he said.

It soon became clear that Mwalimu was right to be cautious. The Minister had to present his budget to Parliament and after writing his budget speech he sent it to me for my comments. On reading it, I found myself in a dilemma because it was full of radical ideas. So I went to Mwalimu and apprised him of the situation. 'I can change it to some extent I but I think it will be very difficult. It really needs to be rewritten,' I told him. Mwalimu then suggested a solution: 'Why don't you tell Mr Hanga that since this is the first time he is presenting this budget, the President himself would like to have a look at his budget speech. Tell him I asked you to inform him of this.' So, Hanga and I went to State House and sat with Mwalimu. After reading the speech, he told Hanga, 'This is an excellent speech but it needs a little bit of adjustment. Perhaps the Minster for Planning could sit down with your two Parliamentary Secretaries and go through the speech. They can fit it in with what we are doing on the mainland currently.' And, of course, by the time we had finished with the text, it was an entirely new speech.

The union of Tanganyika and Zanzibar was achieved in a year when the whole of independent Africa was working towards some degree of unity. On 25 May 1963, in the Ethiopian capital of Addis Ababa, 37 African countries signed the Charter establishing the Organization of African Unity (OAU). The Charter listed the purposes as: promotion of unity and solidarity of the African States; coordination and intensification of their cooperation and efforts to achieve a better life for the peoples of Africa; defence of their sovereignty, their territorial integrity and independence; eradication of all forms of colonialism from Africa; and promotion of international cooperation, with due regard to the Charter of the United Nations and the Universal Declaration of Human Rights.

The African leaders agreed to coordinate and harmonize the general policies of their countries, especially in the following fields: 'political and diplomatic co-operation; economic co-operation, including transport and communications; educational and cultural co-operation; health, sanitation, and nutritional co-operation; scientific and technical co-operation; and co-operation for defence and security'. They declared their adherence to the following principles: the sovereign equality of all member states; non-interference in the internal affairs of states; respect for the sovereignty and territorial integrity of each state and for its inalienable right to independent existence; peaceful settlement of disputes by negotiation, mediation, conciliation or arbitration; unreserved condemnation, in all its forms, of political assassination as well as of subversive activities on the part of neighbouring states or any other state; absolute dedication to the total emancipation of the African territories which were still dependent; affirmation of a policy of non-alignment with regard to all blocs.

There is no doubt in my mind that, had African countries adhered to these principles in practice and carried out their undertakings under the OAU Charter, the history of the continent would have been very different. The history of the OAU has not been total failure, however. It set up a Liberation Committee, which was instrumental in ending apartheid in South Africa. The OAU was also successful in mediating various inter-country and intra-country disputes on the continent.

The independence of Tanganyika and Zanzibar came at a time when the resistance against apartheid policies in South Africa was increasing. The African National Congress (ANC), founded in 1912, had adopted a policy of nonviolent resistance against segregationist laws. In 1958 some members of the ANC had broken away and formed the Pan-African Congress (PAC). In 1960 the PAC organized a demonstration in Sharpeville against laws restricting the movement of black workers in areas reserved for whites. The reaction of the government was extremely brutal: the police fired on the protesters and 69 people were killed. The ANC, PAC and Communist Party were declared illegal. The ANC and PAC then organized guerrilla groups to wage an armed struggle. In 1963, all the main ANC leaders, including Nelson Mandela, were arrested and imprisoned.

Having won freedom from Britain, Mwalimu Nyerere was determined that Tanganyika should help Africans who were still colonized to achieve their own freedom as well, a policy which was continued after the union with Zanzibar. Among the countries that received substantial help were South Africa and Mozambique. An important aspect of this help was in education – providing people with the skills that would be necessary once the struggle was won. South Africans and Mozambicans were given scholarships to study in Tanzanian universities. For example, at one time half of the student intake of Sokoine University of Agriculture (SUA) in Morogoro, of which I am now the Chancellor, was made up of South Africans. The Mozambique Liberation Front (Frelimo) was founded in Dar es Salaam on 25 June 1962 with the merger of the Mozambique African National Union, National Democratic Union of Mozambique and National African Union of Independent Mozambique.

Tanzanians were very happy when Kenya became independent on 12 December 1963, one year after Uganda, which became independent on 9 October 1962. I attended the Independence Day ceremonies in Nairobi as part of His Highness the Aga Khan's delegation and met senior government Ministers. Later, I got to know the Minister for Economic Planning and Development, Tom Mboya, during his visits to Dar es Salaam. He struck me as a bright and aggressive young man. He was full of vigour, eager to build the economy and to improve the living standards of people in Kenya quickly and efficiently. It was with great sadness that I heard the news of his assassination in a Nairobi street on 5 July 1969. Perhaps he had been perceived as being too bright and ambitious by some people.

On 20 May 1963, Mahdi Elmandjra, Chief of the African Section, Bureau of Relations with Member States, Unesco, wrote to me that he would be leaving his post and suggesting that I apply for it through governmental channels. 'Although I am not authorized by the Director-General to make any formal promise, I can assure you that your candidature would be most sympathetically examined along with all the other applications which will be received,' he wrote. I discussed the matter with Mwalimu Nyerere and we decided that at that stage I was needed in Tanganyika and should not apply for the Unesco position.

In 1964, the Director-General of Unesco, René Maheu, wrote a letter to Mwalimu, asking for me to be allowed to join Unesco for two years. He pointed out that it would give me further international exposure. This time, Mwalimu agreed to release me for two years and told me to submit my resignation. On 31 May 1965, accepting my resignation, he confirmed his agreement in the following official letter:

I wish to thank you for your letter of resignation of May 25th, 1965, and also to congratulate you on your new U.N.E.S.C.O. appointment.

I am also glad to be able to grant you formal permission to resign as Parliamentary Secretary of the Ministry of Industries, Mineral Resources and Power, with effect from June 30th, 1965, and to leave Dar es Salaam on or about June 15th.

Needless to say your departure is a great loss not only for me but also for my colleagues in Government, and to our nation as a whole. Ever since I have known you, long before 1958 when I invited you to stand for election, you have shown great determination, diligence and deep devotion to the task of building our nation, and we shall miss you when you go.

However, this appointment is important and it is only for two years. My thoughts will be with you during these two years and I can assure you of a warm welcome when you join us again in our nation-building struggle.

I wish you all the best, and God's speed in all you will be doing in your new office.

So, I went to Paris and began my career at Unesco on 1 July 1965. About 1500 people worked at the Unesco headquarters. The building, which is in Place de Fontenoy, is unique and stands as a landmark in Paris. It is festooned with international flags and generally has a very cosmopolitan ambience. I was on the fifth floor, in the Bureau of Relations with International Organizations and Programmes, which was part of the Office of the Director-General. My job title was Senior Liaison Officer. The Director of the Bureau was a Frenchman, Paul Bertrand, and the Chief of my Division was a Panamanian, Arturo de la Guardia. All my colleagues spoke English, so my lack of French was not a problem. I had hoped that I would be able to learn French during my stay in Paris, but the long hours – we normally worked till 7 p.m. or 8 p.m. – made it impossible. I made many friends, with whom I still exchange Christmas cards regularly. A Deputy Director-General named Adiseshiah, who came from southern India, used to tease me about having been a minister, claiming that I was putting on airs because of it. However, as we got to know each other, the teasing ceased. I also made friends within the Ismaili community in Paris and had the good fortune of visiting His Highness Prince Karim Aga Khan at his residence several times.

My work turned out to be stimulating indeed. As I wrote to Mwalimu on 14 January 1966:

The work itself has been extremely interesting in the past six months because I was doing something new almost every day and because of the variety of problems that one had to face. I hope that the next 18 months will be as invigorating, but I have my doubts because I am not a very good bureaucrat and have a feeling that that is the sort of situation I might find myself in before long.

Fortunately, my fears proved to be unfounded. One of the issues on which I concentrated a lot was adult literacy, trying to get financing for it in various parts of the world. I was responsible for Unesco's relations with the UN Expanded Programme of Technical Assistance in New York. This meant coordinating Unesco's activities in the field of education with various other UN Agencies. These included the Food and Agricultural Organization and the International Labour Organization, both of which had training projects. I would sit down periodically with their people so that we could harmonize our programmes. I also persuaded the UN Development Programme in New York and the World Bank in Washington to finance various Unesco projects.

I kept in regular contact with Mwalimu, updating him on my work and sending him relevant information. For example, on 18 August 1966 I wrote to him, *inter alia*:

I should like to say that the Tanzanian delegation at ECOSOC [UN Economic and Social Council] made quite an impact and was considered to be extremely forceful. The combination of Mwaluko and Waldron-Ramsay was a very good one in that in Mwaluko you have a person who made very statesmanlike, restrained and effective speeches and in Waldron-Ramsay you have an orator who had everyone's ear and who spoke in a most captivating manner. It was obvious from the atmosphere at ECOSOC that this team had made the presence of

Tanzania felt and rarely was there a resolution in which Tanzania was not included as co-sponsor. Having made this initial impact, I believe we might now 'cash in' on our reputation and that technical assessments of some of the less political items of the agenda would be advantageous, so that the maximum benefit is gained, not only by Tanzania, but all the developing countries.

With regard to Tanzania's Unesco programme, I believe the two Special Fund projects which we now have – the Faculty of Science project at the University College and the recently approved Work-Oriented Adult Literacy project for the Lake 'regions' – provide a good nucleus for the present. I believe that there is a further Special Fund project for a Technical Teacher Training Institute which needs to be developed. This project was referred to in the Aide-Memoire of the Deputy Director-General's visit to Dar es Salaam in November last year. Much, of course, will depend, not on getting the project, but on what priority we, in Tanzania, attach to this in relation to other Special Fund projects that we have in mind and for which other international organizations would be the executing agencies. At the moment, I think a Tanzanian request for the establishment of a National Industrial Apprenticeship Scheme is being considered by the UNDP.

On the question of the Expanded Programme of Technical Assistance, the submissions which our Government sent to New York and those relating to Unesco through Paris will be finalized in November when the Governing Council of the UNDP meets. This again will be considered in the light of the priority that our co-ordinating authority, the Treasury I believe, has attached to the various projects in relation to a country target of $1,250,000 that has been proposed for Tanganyika with a further addition of $299,000 for Zanzibar for the 1967-68 biennium [...]

Much as I liked my work at Unesco, I was ready to serve my country in any other capacity, as I informed Mwalimu:

As things stand, I should be completing my work here in the middle of next year and I hope to be back in Dar es Salaam by the first week of October 1967. It is obviously premature for me to ask what plans, if any, you have for me for the future. I should, however, like to say that I look forward to serving Tanzania. In my humble way, I consider your leadership with the highest esteem and I shall treat with honour any services that may be asked of me.

Among other things, I participated in conferences of the UN Economic and Social Council and the UN's Administrative Committee on Coordination. It seems that my participation in these conferences in Geneva and New York got me noticed and the Paris office received reports that I was a good speaker and should be given more responsibility where my oratory skill would be useful. At the end of 1966, René Maheu asked me if I would like to head Unesco's Liaison Office at the United Nations in New York since the current Director, A. Gagliotti, had resigned. I accepted and took up the position in January 1967. The job involved making many public speeches and I felt right in my element.

4

ARUSHA DECLARATION

In February 1967, TANU issued the Arusha Declaration (a copy of which was sent to me in New York) declaring its policy as being to construct a socialist state 'in which neither Capitalism nor Feudalism exist'. This meant a society that was not divided into 'a lower class consisting of people who work for their living, and an upper class consisting of those who live on other people's labour'. Tanzania would be a country where 'everybody who is able to work does so and gets a fair income for his labour, and incomes do not differ substantially'. TANU expressed determination 'to ensure that the major means of production are under the control and ownership of the Peasants and the Workers themselves through their Government and their Co-operatives'.

Observing that Tanzania was a poor country and that dependence on foreign aid for development would endanger its sovereignty, the Arusha Declaration called for a policy of self-reliance:

 Independence cannot be real if a Nation depends upon gifts and loans from another for its development. Even if there was a Nation, or Nations, prepared to give us all the money we need for our development, it would be improper for us to accept such assistance without asking ourselves how this would affect our independence and our very survival as a nation.

TANU also ruled out large-scale foreign investment as the main source of development:

Had we been able to attract investors from America and Europe to come and start all the industries and all the projects of economic development that we need in this country, could we have done so without questioning ourselves? Would we have agreed to leave the economy of our country in the hands of foreigners who would take the profits back to their countries? Supposing they did not insist on taking their profits away, but decided to reinvest them in Tanzania. Would we accept this situation without asking ourselves what disadvantages it would have for our Nation?

The ruling party declared the emphasis on industry and urban development a wrong basis for development. In view of the country's poverty, there was no way to raise the resources needed for industrial development on a substantial enough scale to benefit rural Tanzanians as well. Moreover, urban development was being achieved through loans which were then being repaid with the foreign currency earned through agricultural exports. Thus, the people benefiting from industrialization and urban growth were doing so at the expense of the rural population:

> It means that the people who benefit directly from development which is brought about by borrowed money are not the ones who will repay the loans. The largest proportion of the loans will be spent in, or for, the urban areas, but the largest proportion of the repayment will be made through the efforts of the farmers.

The Arusha Declaration said agriculture should be the foundation of Tanzania's development.

Within a week, the government nationalized banks and some large companies in the milling and wholesale trade sectors. It promised 'full and fair compensation for the assets acquired'. The National Insurance Corporation, in which the government already had a majority shareholding, was nationalized and all new insurance business was to be handled by it. In addition, the government identified several companies in which it intended to hold a controlling share.

In a statement published in the press on 12 February 1967, Mwalimu Nyerere made it clear that Tanzania was not against foreign aid per se:

> 'We shall not depend upon overseas aid to the extent of bending our political, economic or social policies in the hope of getting it. But we shall try to get it in order that we may hasten

our economic progress, and that it may act as a catalyst to our own effort.'

The government's stand on private enterprise was similar: 'We have rejected the domination of private enterprise; but we shall continue to welcome private investment in all those areas not reserved for Government in the Arusha Declaration.'

In a statement published on 14 February 1967, Mwalimu laid to rest any misconceptions that Tanzania's socialist policy was racialist:

Some years ago I made the point that fascism and racialism can go together, but socialism and racialism are incompatible. The reason is easy to see. Fascism is the highest and most ruthless form of the exploitation of man by man; it is made possible by deliberate efforts to divide mankind and set one group of men against another group. In Nazi Germany the majority were incited to join in hostile actions against the Jews – who were a minority religious and ethnic group living among them. 'I hate Jews' became the basis of life for supporters of the Nazi Government. But the man or woman who hates 'Jews', or 'Asians', or 'Europeans', or even 'West Europeans and Americans' is not a Socialist. He is trying to divide mankind into groups and is judging men according to the skin colour and shape they were given by God. Or he is dividing men according to national boundaries. In either case he is denying the equality and brotherhood of man. Without an acceptance of human equality there can be no socialism.

Mwalimu said no race had a monopoly on capitalist attitudes:

Indeed, nobody who was at Arusha needs any more proof that the temptations of capitalism ignore colour boundaries. Even leaders of TANU were getting deeply involved in the practices of capitalism and landlordism. A few had started talking of 'my Company'. And very many others would have done so if they could: they were capitalists by desire even when they could not be so in practice.

He cautioned that 'to try and divide up the people working for our nation into groups of "good" and "bad" according to their skin colour, or their national origin, or their tribal origin, is to sabotage the work we have just embarked on.'

When I first heard of the Arusha Declaration, it was through distorted reports from other people and the media. What I heard and read confused me. It was only when I obtained a copy of the Declaration and read it for myself that I realized that for the most part there was nothing new in it. TANU had always said that it intended Tanzanian society to be based on equality in all fields. The only new aspect was the use of the term 'nationalization', and that was a logical extension of TANU's creed. I was not sure what the future would bring to Tanzanians but I was willing to give the party the benefit of the doubt. As I wrote to Mwalimu:

> As you know, I was brought up in a rather peculiar way, and so many accidents have taken place in my own little life that I tended to accept each stage as it presented itself. I have never done any serious political studies, nor have I ever had pretensions of being an exponent of one ideology or another. My love of and belief in Tanzania and my highest respect for you are such that I shall continue to do whatever I feel, to the extent of my ability, is in the interest of Tanzania and its people.

I was also glad that my family would not be affected, since we owned no industries.

Some Members of the National Assembly raised interesting questions about the Arusha Declaration, and I found the answers given by Mwalimu thought-provoking. Most of the questions related to Part Five of the Declaration, which enjoined that every TANU and government leader should be either a peasant or a worker, and in no way be associated with the practices of capitalism or feudalism; that no leader should hold shares in any company, no leader should hold directorships in any privately owned enterprises, no leader should receive two or more salaries and no leader should own houses rented to others.

The term 'leader' was defined as comprising 'members of the TANU National Executive Committee; ministers, members of parliament, senior officials of organisations affiliated to TANU, senior officials of parastatal organisations, all those appointed or elected under any clause of the TANU constitution, councillors, and civil servants in high and middle cadres'. 'Leader' was specifically defined as ' a man, or a man and his wife; a woman, or a woman and her husband'.

This resolution of the TANU Executive Committee seemed to worry some Members of the National Assembly. For example, one Member asked, 'If a man sells his second house, what does he do with the money if he is not allowed to invest it and enjoy the income from the investment?' Mwalimu's reply was, 'Any TANU and Government leader who sells a house or houses may invest the money by putting it in the Bank, by putting it in Post Office Savings, by buying Tanzania Government Stock from the Bank, or by saving through a Savings and Credit Society. On all these things he gets interest; he may receive that interest – and enjoy it.' Thus, income from rent and private sector stocks was wrong, but there was no problem with income from Government stocks and interest on savings.

Another question referred to the change in the property market: 'Due to the Arusha Declaration, property values have gone down in Dar es Salaam; also there is a reluctance on the part of buyers to invest in property. If a man cannot sell his house before the end of the "year of grace", even though he tries hard to do so, what is he to do?' The reply was blunt:

Before the Arusha Declaration speculators, and others who were able to borrow money, were exploiting the shortage of houses in Dar es Salaam and were charging exorbitant rents or selling at a huge profit. One good thing which the Arusha Declaration has already done is to bring prices down to a more reasonable level. But even if they fall further, no house is likely to have a sale price lower than its cost price – and prices will almost certainly continue to allow some profit. However little that profit is, it should be remembered that the owner has done nothing to earn it; he has obtained money just by being one of the few who were able to borrow the money necessary to build.

Before anyone says they have been unable to sell their extra house, we should want to know what price he was trying to obtain for it. We certainly hope that there will be no success for the person who left Arusha and instructed his contractor to sell for £20,000 the house which had cost him £7,500.

If, however, despite the shortage of houses in Dar es Salaam and elsewhere, a leader does not succeed in selling his house, he has an easy way out in almost all cases. He can surrender the house to the organisation which has a mortgage on it, i.e., the organisation which lent him the money. Government will then consider in each individual case whether they should refund the money he paid to obtain the plot and the designs.

A Member raised the question of fairness: 'If a man has taken the lump sum pension he received after 15 years' service in the British Civil Service, and has invested that money in a house which he lets out, is it just to ask him to sell that house?' The reply was:

If the man in question has no intention of holding a leadership position, either in the Party or in the Government, it would be unjust to ask him to sell his house. No one is asking, or will ever ask, that he should do this. If, on the other hand, he wants a leadership position in the Party or the Government, it is definitely not unjust to ask him to behave like 99.9 per cent of the people whom he says he wants to lead or serve. They feel themselves to be lucky if they have a house of their own to live in – at least in the urban areas. Real leadership demands understanding and identification; this cannot be achieved while the leader is in a position which enables exploitation. And although the man in this case originally earned his pension, he may be accused of using his reward for exploitative purposes.

It is important to be clear about this. Even if the individual is in fact receiving no more than a fair interest on his money – that is, no more than the Bank or Government would give – there are two other factors to be considered. The first is that he, a leader, will be in a position where he controls the shelter of another individual, who is probably not a leader and who might consequently feel himself at a disadvantage in any negotiations. The second is that either his tenant, or other people, may fail to understand that the rent being charged is a fair one so that they will believe him to be exploiting them even if he is not. A leader should not voluntarily get into such a position ; it should be absolutely obvious that he is not in a position to exploit another human being.

So, leaders had to set an example and avoid acting in any way that could be interpreted as not being socialist.

Another Member felt that the ban on rental income would put Africans at a disadvantage: 'If a man is not allowed to invest in property by building and renting out a house, is this not barring Africans from participating in the development of Dar es Salaam and other towns, and handing this development over to Asians and foreigners? Is this right or wise?' Mwalimu saw through the questioner's motives and did not mince his words:

This is an old trick. It is the appeal to racialism by a selfish minority, which hopes to confuse the majority and thus secure benefit for themselves. The Arusha Declaration does not stop the activities of African capitalists, or would-be African capitalists, any more then it stops other capitalists, be they European or Asian. What the Arusha Declaration does is to say that if Africans or any other Tanzania Citizens choose to be capitalists, then they must forfeit their right to lead a Socialist Party or hold a position of responsibility in a Government committed to Socialist objectives.

People who raise this question in these racial terms are really saying that they want the Party to install them as exploiters of the masses rather than leave the old exploiters, the majority of whom, in Tanzania, happened to come from the Asian community. The Arusha Declaration is a declaration of war on exploitation; it is not just a declaration of war on those exploiters who happen to be of a different colour. Does the man whose goods are being sucked through a *mirija* [straw] care what colour the suckers are? He is concerned to get rid of the *mirijas*; he will not be made any better off if he is told that the old suckers have been got rid of and the new suckers are black.

Some people seem to want it both ways. They want the opportunity to exploit the people, and at the same time they want the right to serve the people and lead them in the struggle against exploitation. They try to justify this contradiction on the grounds that they are black! They say 'the poor are black, and we are black, therefore it is alright for us to exploit them'. But instead of putting it in these terms, when the masses would immediately understand, they try to confuse the people by pretending that there is something more evil in a brown or white Tanzanian doing the exploiting than there is in a black Tanzanian doing it.

The Arusha Declaration applies to all leaders, whatever their colour. It applies to the Councillors of Dar es Salaam who are of Asian origin as much as those who are of African origin. The Arusha Declaration is in conformity with the first statement of belief in the TANU Constitution, which says: 'I believe in the brotherhood of man [...]' Those who try to undermine the Arusha Declaration by appealing to racialism in the manner of this question are showing that they do not accept that first TANU principle.

Providing financial security also became an issue: 'How is a man to get security for his wife and children in the event of his death if he is not allowed to invest for them or save for them?' Mwalimu replied:

The Arusha Declaration opposes exploitation. And exploitation is still exploitation even if it is undertaken with the intention of assisting one's children. Every millionaire in America will tell you that he is concerned to give a good inheritance for his children – and it will be true. It is wrong for a man to provide security for his wife and children by exploiting other men, women and children. Let a man work. Let his wife work. Let them save some of their income and put it in a Bank where it will earn interest. These savings will help towards security in the case of accidents. And this applies to everybody; it is therefore fair – although the vast majority of our people will still find it difficult even to put anything in the savings banks because they have so little to live on.

One day in the future the State will be able to provide old age pensions for everybody, and have widows and orphans insurance schemes for all. At present these are provided for only a tiny minority of wage earners, and especially civil servants. What this question is asking is why some of these same people, plus a few politicians, should not be allowed to achieve even more for themselves even if it means exploiting the people to achieve it. This is exactly what the Arusha Declaration will not allow. It denies the right of any leader in Party or Government to achieve security for himself at the cost of the people he is leading.

A similar question was asked with regard to children: 'How can a man guarantee education for his children in the event of his death or loss of job if he cannot invest his savings?' Mwalimu demolished the argument:

This is another attempt to justify exploitation by an appeal to the sentiment of children's welfare. Children's welfare is of vital importance to every parent, and to every good Tanzania citizen. But to the Government and Party leaders every Tanzanian child ought to be of equal importance. Certainly there can be no justification for exploiting one child's father in order that another child's father may make provision for insecurity. In any case, it is absurd to use the question of education as an excuse for exploitation.

Which leader in Tanzania has been guaranteeing the education of his children through his own savings and investments? Even where parents are asked to make a small contribution to primary school costs by payment of a 'fee', the real costs are met by the taxpayers. Something like Shs. 10 million was received in 1965 in primary school fees; Central Government alone paid Shs. 47,000,000 and Local Governments paid Shs. 39,000,000. These taxes are paid by everyone – including some parents who can find no school places for their children. And all Secondary education and University education in Tanzania is paid for by the taxpayer.

The only time Tanzanians pay for the education of their children is if they decide to buy privilege for them. That is, if the child does not succeed in the competition for a secondary school place, then there are a few 'private schools' where fees are high – and the education of varying quality. If a capitalist decides he is willing to pay these fees, he is simply living up to his own creed – and we are not stopping him from doing so. But for a leader of a Socialist Party to try to justify the exploitation of people in order to give a special advantage to his own child is inconsistent in the extreme. A leader in TANU should recognize that, even while he has a special emotional feeling for his own child, he has an equal responsibility for all the children of the people he represents.

Then there was a question about security in old age: 'How can a man make provision for his old age when he is too old to farm?' It received short shrift:

How do the people who elected the MPs make provision for their old age? Why should a TANU leader be any different? What is there which is so special about his case? The only special thing is that he receives, at least for five years, an income of £700 a year, plus allowances, as a reward for representing the people. Almost none of the people he represents will ever receive so much, however hard they work. They will be lucky if they receive in a lifetime what he receives in five years.

One Member was worried about the economic insecurity of a political career:

A politician has no security. Today he is a Minister, tomorrow not; today he is an MP, after five years he is not; today he is a Regional Commissioner or Area Commissioner, tomorrow he is unemployed; today he is Chairman of the Region, District, or Town, and tomorrow someone else may be elected in his place. Why does the Arusha Declaration prevent such leaders from providing by other means for their future?

Mwalimu termed the question dangerous, because, among other things, it implied that a leader should be allowed to exploit his position:

What other means? Leaders ask this question more than any other question, and it is the most serious and dangerous question of all. The Arusha Declaration says that a TANU leader will be a peasant or worker. Before he is chosen as a leader he will be working as a peasant, working for wages, or working on his own account as a carpenter, blacksmith, goldsmith, etc. This is the work by which he meets his needs now, and through which he prepares for his future security. When he asks the people to give him the responsibilities of leadership, this job will be one of two kinds. Either it will be the kind which does not require full-time work, in which case he may be able to continue with his normal way of earning a living, or it will be a full-time leadership position which will require him to leave his normal employment. For example, a Minister or an Area Commissioner could not continue to be a carpenter or farmer. He must leave this work in order to fulfil his leadership responsibilities properly. But the cell leader, District Councillor, or Regional Chairman would not have to abandon his farm or his carpentering completely, because these are not full-time positions.

Leaders who are required to do full-time work are paid wages for their positions – some are paid a small wage and some have a bigger wage, but all are given wages which are good in comparison with the general standard of living in Tanzania. Very often these wages enable a leader to live at a higher standard than he did before getting his leadership position.

Tomorrow or the day after this leader can leave or can be dismissed from his leadership. If he is dismissed after he has held the job for only a short time, he will be able to return to his previous employment without difficulty, or if he does not wish to do this he can find another job like any other worker. Let us not forget that leaving a job, or being dismissed from it, is not something which arises just out of the Arusha Declaration; it is a quite ordinary thing in our country. It was only very recently that our TANU Government passed a law forcing employers to pay severance allowance to those whom they had dismissed when the worker was not at fault. And even now workers are still dismissed and have to find other jobs. And even although such a worker may have severance pay, and a dismissed politician does not, the severance pay really cannot be said to be sufficient to take care of the worker's whole future. And as we shall see below, the politician has a much better chance of safeguarding the future from his leadership income than has an ordinary worker.

If a man leaves or is dismissed from his leadership position after he has had it for a long time, he is still able to look for work like everyone else, even if he cannot return to his old job. But more than that, while he was in this leadership position the workers have paid him a wage which was large enough to enable him to save at least something for the future. Rather than grumbling at the people, such leaders ought to thank the people very much for paying them enough to save, while the people themselves do not have enough income to be able to do so.

The other kind of leader is he whose job did not make him leave his normal work. For example, a Civil Servant who is chosen as a street cell leader; he did not have to leave his employment in order to be a cell leader because this is not a full-time job; it is something he is doing to serve the country. The same thing applies to a factory worker who is chosen as a Town Councillor, or a farmer who is chosen as a Member or Chairman of his district or village. Such people can just carry on with their normal work if they cease to be in their leadership positions, and there is therefore no need to give them any special allowance while they are finding new things to do. Nor can such a leader say that his leadership responsibilities prevented him from providing for his needs or for the future.

But having said all this, let us not forget the most important thing. That is, that leadership is not the work by which a man ought to expect to earn his living and look after his future. The difference between the work of leadership and other kinds of work is that in leadership what is sought is the opportunity to lead and to give leadership which will help the people; the thing which is desired by the 'employer' – that is, the people – is therefore the service of leadership which has fruits for the people – not anything else. The purpose of the kind of leadership we are trying to build up in Tanzania must be the benefit of the people, not the benefit of the leaders themselves. The personal difficulties of the leaders are of interest to the people only to the extent that they might be of such a degree that the leader cannot do his work properly. It is this consideration which causes some leaders to be paid while they carry responsibility. Leaders often forget this, and especially do they tend to forget the purposes of leadership in a socialist Tanzania; it is a good thing if the Arusha Declaration and its leadership requirements act as a constant reminder.

Which is the politician who went to the people at election time and asked them to elect him so that he could provide for his future? Which Area or Regional Commissioner or other TANU worker got his job by saying he wanted to improve his personal position and get security for his future? Whenever a person seeks political work, whether it is through election or by appointment, he says he wants the opportunity to serve the people, to guard their interests and to further their aspirations. What right has such a person, once he has the appointment he sought on this basis, to use his responsibility for his own betterment?

This question is absolutely central to the Arusha Declaration and to the whole purpose of TANU and an independent Tanzania. For the question is asking why a politician may not be allowed to exploit his position, his importance, and the trust which has been placed in him, so that he may himself get security. A simple farmer will not be able to borrow money to build houses which he can then rent out at a profit. Why then should the fact that he has become, for example, an M.P., change the situation? If it does change the situation it means that he is getting the opportunity to exploit people just because of his office, just because he is an M.P.

Mwalimu pointed out that there were underlying motives behind such privileges.

When we were struggling for independence how many of us did the capitalists invite to become directors? How many of us were able to borrow money to build houses for renting out? How many of us were lent money to buy large *shambas* [farms] on which it is necessary to employ labour? If we have acquired these things since independence most of us have done so because the capitalists want to involve us in their system of exploitation so that we shall become defenders of that system. The fact that this question is asked shows that this technique has had some success.

Government and Party leaders should have the same degree of security as the poor peasants and workers we were elected to serve. In fact we have more. For the period we serve we get a much higher salary than those we lead. We are able to save and earn interest on our savings. Then if we are not elected or if we decide not to stand, or if it is decided that we are unfit for the jobs which require to be done, we already have an advantage over those we claim to have been serving. We go around telling the unemployed in towns to go and farm; we go to the peasants and tell them to work harder and with greater expertise. What right have we to tell the peasants and workers to do these things, if when the time comes we are not prepared to practise what we have been preaching?

Any person is allowed under the Arusha Declaration to 'provide for his future' by investing in property. But he cannot do this while he is pretending to lead and serve the people. Let those who are worried about their future resign from their leadership positions and take on other work and exploit the people if they can. In fact very few will be able to do it, because for the vast majority of leaders the only way they can get into a position to exploit their fellows is by taking advantage of their position of responsibility – that is, by misusing it.

Not all the questioners were explicitly critical about the Arusha Declaration. One phrased his question in the form of agreement and a need to improve its implementation: 'Although the Arusha Declarations are basically right, are they not being put into effect too drastically and without thought and planning?' Mwalimu replied:

There is a possible element of truth in the suggestion that we have not done, and are not doing, enough planning to enable all the aspects of the Arusha Declaration to be implemented without some inconvenience and without some mistakes. But this is the responsibility of leadership in Party and Government. In saying this we are criticizing ourselves – or we should be. We must think about the purpose of the Declaration, and the implications of self-reliance, and each one of us should be helping by coming forward with ideas about how it can best become a reality. These ideas should be being discussed now in the Party and in the Government, for if a thing is basically right then it must be put into practice – and quickly.

The trouble is that this question can so easily be, and so often is, used as an excuse for doing nothing. The Bankers are among those who are using this technique; they are saying, 'Why did you not tell us so that we could make plans?' For what does it mean to talk of putting the Arusha Declaration into effect 'drastically'? Either you nationalize or you don't; either you take a majority shareholding or you don't. If you are unemployed and there is no prospect of getting a job tomorrow, either you go out now and employ yourself on the land as the majority of our people do, or you sit around doing nothing. There is no half-way house. In the case of the leaders we have given time, so that if they choose to accept the future conditions of leadership they have an opportunity to clear their affairs.

This talk that something is 'basically right – but' has been applied successfully to every major reform in the history of man. It is always used by privileged people to justify the retention or extension of their privileges. So we have people saying, 'Equality is basically right, but …', 'non-racialism is basically right, but … ', 'caring about the poor is right, but …'. And in the end the 'but' dominates, and the 'basically right' thing goes on being basically right but not getting done. For us in Africa this is a bigger danger than making mistakes of over-enthusiasm.

It was clear that there was unease within the political establishment about losing their privileges. And it was equally clear that Mwalimu was determined that the interests of workers and peasants should be paramount and that there should be no ethnic or racial discrimination in Tanzania. He himself lived a simple life and scrupulously observed the principles set out in the Arusha Declaration. I had never heard him say anything or seen him do anything that violated those principles. Now all the other leaders were expected to do the same.

It was in this context that Tanzania established the Ujamaa villages. The reason for them was explained by Mwalimu in the following way:

It is particularly important that we should now understand the connection between freedom, development, and discipline, because our national policy of creating socialist villages throughout the rural areas depends upon it. For we have known for a very long time that development had to go on in the rural areas, and that this required co-operative activities by the people […].

When we tried to promote rural development in the past, we sometimes spent huge sums of money on establishing a Settlement, and supplying it with modern equipment, and social services, as well as often providing it with a management hierarchy […] All too often, we persuaded people to go into new settlements by promising them that they could quickly grow rich there, or that Government would give them services and equipment which they could not hope to receive either in the towns or in their traditional farming places. In very few cases was any ideology involved; we thought and talked in terms of greatly increased output, and of things being provided for the settlers.

What we were doing, in fact, was thinking of development in terms of things, and not of people [...] As a result, there have been very many cases where heavy capital investment has resulted in no increase in output, where the investment has been wasted. And in most of the officially sponsored or supported schemes, the majority of people who went to settle lost their enthusiasm, and either left the scheme altogether, or failed to carry out the orders of the outsiders who were put in charge – and who were not themselves involved in the success or failure of the project.

It is important, therefore, to realize that the policy of Ujamaa Vijijini [villages] is not intended to be merely a revival of the old settlement schemes under another name. The Ujamaa village is a new conception, based on the post-Arusha Declaration under-standing that what we need to develop is people, not things, and that people can only develop themselves.

There has been criticism that that one of the reasons for Ujamaa villages failing to achieve their aims was that people were forced into them. However, Mwalimu's intention was that villagers should be persuaded – not forced – to participate:

Ujamaa villages are intended to be socialist organizations created by the people, and governed by those who live and work in them. They cannot be created from outside, nor governed from outside. No one can be forced into an Ujamaa village, and no official – at any level – can go and tell the members of an Ujamaa village what they should do together, and what they should continue to do as individual farmers [...].

It is important that these things should be thoroughly understood. It is also important that the people should not be persuaded to start an Ujamaa village by promises of the things which will be given to them if they do so. A group of people must decide to start an Ujamaa village because they have understood that only through this method can they live and develop in dignity and freedom, receiving the full benefits of their co-operative endeavour.

In April 1971, when I was back in Tanzania, the government nationalized all private buildings from which the owners were earning rent in excess of a certain amount. Our family owned many commercial properties in Dar es Salaam, including a very well-known bar and restaurant, the Cosy Café, office and residential buildings, and cinemas. There was a hasty family gathering to discuss the government action. My brothers and I expected our father to be furious about losing the properties he had acquired through hard work over more than half a century. However, he surprised us. 'I am happy the buildings have been nationalized – I will no longer have to pay income tax since I won't be earning rent,' he said with a broad smile.

* * * *

While the momentous changes of the Arusha Declaration were occurring in Tanzania, my job in New York was basically to represent Unesco and keep the Paris headquarters informed of relevant developments. On 10 March 1967, I travelled to Toronto to give the keynote speech at the annual dinner of the Canadian National Commission for Unesco. It was my first visit to Toronto. Normally, whenever I visited a place I made a point of going to the local Ismaili *jamatkhana*, but, as far as I knew, there were only two Ismaili families in the whole of Canada at that time. In Toronto, it was the Niaz Jethwani family, but unfortunately I was unable to get in touch with them. Today, of course, the situation is very different, with the Ismaili population in Canada being about 80,000.

The topic of my speech was the educational revolution in Africa, which I considered just as significant for the continent's future as the political events sweeping through it. In 1961, as the people of Africa were freeing themselves from colonialism country by country, only 16 per cent of school-age children had been attending school, compared with a world average of 48 per cent Only about three per cent had been attending secondary school and less than two per cent were in university. Therefore, it was not surprising that, after independence, educational reform was high on government agendas.

African leaders met in the Ethiopian capital of Addis Ababa in 1961 under the sponsorship of Unesco and the United Nations Economic Commission for Africa to formulate their own educational goals. They called for a doubling of high school education within five years. Enrolment in primary schools was also to be increased by 15 per cent. The leaders hoped that by 1980 there would be universal primary education, with 20 per cent of those who passed the final exams going on to secondary school. The target for secondary school graduates going for higher education was also set at 20 per cent. These goals were incorporated into the Addis Ababa plan.

In March 1962 a conference of Education Ministers of the African countries participating in the execution of the Plan was held at Unesco's Paris headquarters. Thirty-four states and territories of sub-Saharan Africa and four North African countries were represented. The conference recommended improved educational-planning machinery, integrated educational, economic and social planning, expansion of teacher training, priority to secondary education, more attention to rural and adult education, and further research in language teaching.

In the same year a Conference on the Development of Higher Education was held in Tananarive, Madagascar, where the participants discussed the practical problems of adapting curricula to African needs, administration, organization, structure and financing. They noted that the problems in sub-Saharan Africa were worse than those in North Africa and so focused on that part of the continent. The conference identified 32 existing and planned universities on which all resources should be concentrated.

In 1964, African Ministers of Education met again to review progress in implementing the Addis Ababa Plan, this time in Abidjan, capital of Côte d'Ivoire. They agreed that there had been remarkable achievements in primary education but less progress at the secondary school level because of a shortage of qualified teachers. Technical schools and training centres, almost non-existent in 1961, were developing rapidly. Moreover, there were three new universities to add to the list of 32 identified at the Paris conference.

It was in this context that I explained to the Canadian National Commission for Unesco members how Unesco was helping African countries to achieve their educational revolution. A new regional centre had been created at Dakar, Senegal, for educational planning and administration. The World Bank and Unesco were sending joint planning missions to many African countries.

The African countries were facing many hurdles in expanding their educational systems. Unesco was convinced that if education was to be a spontaneous outgrowth of cultural experience and learning rather than an alien graft, the initial education experience should be in the mother tongue of the pupils. However, some African countries had as many as 100 languages, many of which had no written alphabet. In the case of some languages shared by several countries, the opposite problem was encountered. For example, in Northern Nigeria, Hausa was written in the Roman alphabet with English spelling; whereas in Niger it was written in Roman alphabet with French spelling; and elsewhere it was written in Arabic. Unesco was helping African countries with such problems to standardize an alphabet.

As far as the shortage of teachers was concerned, Unesco, with the assistance of the UN Special Fund, had set up secondary school teacher training colleges, which were expected to produce 1500 teachers every year from 1969. It was also providing help to train primary school teachers since about half a million teachers would be needed if the African countries were to realize the goal of universal primary education by 1980. The Swedish government was helping by channelling its bilateral aid to education through Unesco. In addition, Unesco and Unicef were drawing up plans for joint education projects.

Madagascar was experimenting with an interesting example of adapting education to make it relevant to African conditions. To cope with the shortage of teachers, it was using baccalaureate graduates in rural schools. In addition to the usual school curriculum, the pupils also learned agricultural fundamentals. Thus, the morning was devoted to the normal curriculum and in the afternoon the pupils worked in vegetable gardens. In one case, the system was so successful that the pupils' parents started growing the same vegetables and berries on their own land. To encourage the trend, the school arranged for a truck to pick up the parents' produce once a week and take it to the market in Tananarive.

The structure of the primary school system was also different. Pupils attended rural schools for four years, and then the best of them did two more years of what was termed senior primary school, which provided more specialized instruction preparing them for secondary school. Thus, in their formative years children were integrated into the rural economy instead of being isolated from it through a purely academic curriculum. This decreased migration to urban areas and consequent overwhelming of the infrastructure and services there.

I emphasized to my audience:

The curriculum and teaching in Africa *must* be Africanized. By that we do not mean that we plan to throw away the riches of Western culture, thought and science. But to appreciate them fully we must also know and nurture our own writers, poets and artists. We have them, as you know so well. But we must be sure that our children grow up in schools where pride in our own accomplishments is not stifled and where, being proud of their own, they can in turn love yours the more.

Africanization has particular relevance in scientific subjects. Today, some African children are still learning dissection from dogfish shipped from Europe, and botany from lichens and moss which do not grow in Africa. A major effort is being made to provide materials generic to the area.

Africanization should in no way be construed to mean a lowering of standards. Whatever else is put on the debit side of the balance sheet for colonial rule in Africa, on the credit side will always remain the fact that both Britain and France attached a guarantee of standards when they brought universities to Africa. They did not export a cheap version. Now, by slow and natural growth, these universities are assuming their own identities, seeking to retain their academic worth and standards while at the same time introducing more and more of Africa into their teaching – no easy task since many of the books are only starting to be written now, and research is in its primary stages.

As one African official put it, 'Universities serve their purpose only if they fulfil a dual loyalty: to their own people and society, and to the world standards of higher education. If the first fails, the university serves only an esoteric elite. This can happen only too easily and must be carefully guarded against. If the second loyalty fails, the consequences are even worse. The people, including the educated elite, will limp behind the rest of the world.'

Today, unfortunately, it is still possible, as a senior education officer in Uganda said, for an African to graduate from university with a good B.A. knowing practically nothing about the complicated social structure of his own people. Fascinating and intricate networks of organization exist among some of

Africa's peoples. They include a sliding scale of local taxes according to the number of canoes a man owns, the close clan affinities and systems of justice among the Bantu people, the ingenious systems of checks and balances among other tribes to protect them from autocracy. In West Africa, the Yorubas have their own intricate economies for trading, the Ibos their own particular laws of ownership and inheritance. All of this is not just interesting antiquarian lore, it is almost essential knowledge for the African intellectual, civil servant or teacher who must face the responsibility of leading his own people from the old Africa to the new – an Africa where the unity of its people is fostered by a genuine understanding of the people.

Unesco was helping in this process. It had established a textbook production centre in the Cameroon, which was printing a steady stream of new, fresh textbooks written by African writers, in indigenous languages, geared to the child's environment and aspirations. The aim was to turn over the production of textbooks to local printers as soon as they were able to take it over. To fulfil this aim, the centre was training printers, bookbinders, editorial workers and production staff for the region. Unesco was also helping African countries to prepare a major history of the continent which could serve as a source for textbook writers.

In addition, Africa faced a severe infrastructure problem: to achieve the aims of the Addis Ababa Plan, the continent needed to build half a million new classrooms within 15 years; this at a time when many rural schools were holding classes out in the open in the shade of fruit trees. Unesco's School Building Centre in Khartoum had found that in most parts of Africa, the continent's predominant soil, red laterite, when mixed with cement in a 10 to 1 ratio, made a reasonable building brick and that was being used to build schools.

Africa needed to increase the literacy rate urgently and could not afford to wait while schools were being built and furnished and teachers trained to educate the next generation. Among the population over 15 years of age, the illiteracy rate was between 80 and 85 per cent in some areas. Increasing the literacy rate, of course, had its own problems, as exemplified by one husband in a North African town who was refusing to let his wife learn to read and write. The teacher, trying to get him to change his mind, pointed out that if his wife attended literacy classes she would be able to write her own letters. 'To whom?' asked the irate husband!

To raise the literacy rate in Africa as quickly as possible as well as speed up economic growth, Unesco and the UN Development Programme had launched a major campaign to link literacy to economic development. For example, 100,000 farmers growing rice and cotton along the Niger River were to be given literacy lessons in their cooperatives; this was to be coupled with an intensive programme in new agricultural techniques, including proper use of fertilizers. In Mali, the World Food Programme was providing an incentive by giving food to adults attending evening literacy classes. In Bamako, workers living in the industrial zone were to receive intensive literacy and vocational training for two hours every day for nine months. The teachers would be unpaid volunteers trained by Unesco, which also provided audiovisual equipment to make the lessons interesting. Mobile library units were set up to provide books at various industrial centres. The Mali programme was a pilot study, to be duplicated elsewhere in future. Similar projects were under way in Tanzania.

Africa's biggest overall problem was that it could not afford to develop at the same rate as Europe had developed – over centuries. And faster progress, of course, would require vast amounts of funding. External assistance was vital. That was where Canada came in, I told my audience.

You are aware, I am sure, of Canada's advantages respective of overseas aid. As one of your own great educators, Dr. Roby Kidd, has pointed out, you share the knowhow and knowledge of the West but are not stigmatized as are the larger, more powerful nations. You possess the two languages, French and English, which beyond all others are essential for international communication, particularly in Africa.

You have vigorously supported Unesco's work in Africa. Canadians who have served there in a private capacity have done well too – the names of Margaret Wrong, Father Matte and Cran Pratt are known to thousands. And another Canadian, a brave young teacher, Noëlla Lahaie, started the first girls' school in the bush in Garango, Upper Volta. She, with two other young Canadians, started where there were, as she put it, 'No desks, no blackboards, no books, no notebooks! Nothing but ten fingers. Plus ten sentences painfully spoken in Bisa […]. And, of course, my experience teaching in Canada.' Working in temperatures up to 110 degrees in the shade, these Canadians have – with patience and imagination – created a fine school, which is serving as a model throughout the entire area. These are a few. Many are needed, and will be needed for years to come.

I observed that the Swedish government, using Unesco as its executive agency, 'has already set a pattern of aid which African nations hope other countries will follow, through helping women's education in Tanzania, Sierra Leone, Kenya, Uganda and Ghana.' Such aid would not be a one-way flow. 'You in turn will be enriched – by Africa's art, her writers, her poets, her spontaneity, her great riches waiting to be tapped.' I pointed out that, 'at a time when science is opening the gateway to stars it is unthinkable that two-fifths of mankind should be prisoners of ancestral darkness.'

As the end of my contract with Unesco approached, I received a message from Martin Hill, Assistant Secretary-General for Inter-Agency Affairs in the UN. He informed me that the UN Secretary-General U Thant had said he was very impressed with my work and would I like to join the UN as Secretary of the Economic and Social Council (ECOSOC)? I replied that my contract with Unesco only had a few months to go and I would check with President Nyerere to see if my stay in New York could be extended. In reply to my letter, Mwalimu said I should accept the post for two years. So, on 1 July I took up my new position at the United Nations headquarters. The head of ECOSOC, UN Under-Secretary-General Philippe de Seynes, had a discussion over lunch with René Maheu in New York to arrange for me to be released from Unesco. Maheu jokingly complained to him that he had identified me as somebody whose talent would be useful to the UN system and de Seynes was stealing me away from him.

All international nongovernmental organizations (NGOs) in the world registered with ECOSOC, and as its Secretary I once addressed a conference of 158 national, regional and international NGOs on 'Trade, Aid and People in an Interdependent World' at the UN Headquarters. My speech focused on why trade is preferable to aid. I emphasized the importance of self-respect and dignity to developing nations and that they should not be treated as beggars. Instead, they should be helped through trade to develop their economies, enabling them to achieve economic growth through their

The author with UN Secretary-General U Thant at a meeting in Rome of the UN Administrative Committee on Coordination, May 1969.

own efforts. A more equal relationship of economic negotiation and trade would also fit in better with the preferences of developed nations.

Also, I noted, the economic effects of aid are less satisfactory than those of trade, since inflation continually undermines aid. The economic spiral created by inflation eats away at the aid received by developing countries in the same way that a tax increase reduces the effects of a rise in income. Thus, I said, while developed countries had been generous in providing aid, the productivity of that assistance in terms of overall gains was questionable.

In contrast, trade assistance in the form of higher prices for commodities produced by the developing nations would be much more fruitful. Its economic benefits would not be affected by inflation. Improved terms of trade would be of long-term benefit. They would also be relatively painless for the developed countries. For example, a slight rise in the price of a cup of coffee as a result of coffee farmers receiving more for their crop would be resisted less by consumers than a tax increase to provide more foreign aid. Moreover, improvement in the incomes of people in developing countries would ultimately be beneficial to developed countries as well, because it would result in a bigger market for the products of industrialized countries. I quoted Paul Hoffman (head of the United Nations Development Programme): 'Poor countries make poor customers.' Of course, to make trade possible, aid would still be necessary in the short term, but it should be aid to help developing countries acquire technical knowhow: 'If you give a man a fish, you feed him for a day. If you teach him *how* to fish, he can feed himself for a lifetime.'

The speech was well received and many of the delegates later sent me letters of congratulation.

In addition to the ECOSOC position, I was also Secretary of the Administrative Committee on Coordination, which was made up of the heads of the specialized agencies and was chaired by U Thant. In addition, I was Secretary of the Second Committee of the UN General Assembly, which handled economic and social affairs.

One of the most important things I did at ECOSOC was to help draft the resolution leading to the UN Conference on the Human Environment, which was held in Stockholm in June 1972. The event was important not only as a major turning point in global efforts to reduce environmental degradation but also because it was the stimulation for the creation of a UN agency that would focus on environmental issues. The subject was then discussed by the UN General Assembly in New York and the UN Environmental Programme (UNEP) was established in Nairobi that same year, with Maurice Strong as its first Executive Director. Under him, UNEP successfully raised international consciousness about the need to protect the environment.

Towards the end of 1969, U Thant's Chef de Cabinet, C.V. Narasimhan, told me, 'Would you like to come and join us?' I said, 'What do you mean, us?' He replied, 'On the thirty-eighth floor. I would like you to become Director of U Thant's Executive Office.' I pointed out that the extension granted to me by President Nyerere would soon be up, so I could not take up the offer. He said, 'Do you want me to write to him?' I said, 'You write to him.' Then he said, Do you mind if U Thant writes as well?' So, on 12 December 1969, I wrote a letter to President Nyerere:

> From the letter which U Thant is writing to you and which will be delivered at the same time as this one, you will see that he would like me to work for him on the 38th floor.
>
> I was quite taken aback by the proposal and for the past 48 hours my mind has been in a complete whirl.
>
> In recent weeks I have been making preparations for my imminent return to Tanzania and, as you know from my previous letters, I am anxious to return. Indeed, if it was simply a question of personal choice, I would rather come home and work in the post that you have in mind for me. On the other hand, if, as a result of what the Secretary-General has to say, you feel that I ought to accept the offer and stay on for a while at the United Nations, I would be perfectly willing to do so.
>
> If on the basis of our own priorities and commitments at home you find it necessary to decline U Thant's request, I am sure he will understand.

The letter from the UN Secretary-General to Mwalimu was also dated 12 December 1969 :

> I have learned that Mr. Al Noor Kassum, the Secretary of the Economic and Social Council, is planning to leave us soon in order to return home to work for the Tanzanian Government.

Needless to say, we should be extremely sorry to see him go, as he has served the cause of the United Nations well in his present capacity and has impressed both my colleagues and me as a person of considerable potential and one who is dedicated to the aims and purposes which we are all striving to attain.

I well understand the needs of States such as yours for men of his calibre, and Mr. Kassum's desire to contribute in whatever measure he can to the development of his own country, but I venture all the same to write to you at this juncture. I have informed Mr. Kassum that I believe he would be well suited to fill a high post now vacant in my Executive Office. Quite understandably, he is most reluctant to consider the proposal unless it has your full support. He has given me to understand that he believes plans to be fairly well advanced for his proposed assignment in Tanzania, and that it may be difficult for you to release him at this stage. If this is so, I shall, of course, accept your decision. If, however, you could see your way to spare him at least until the end of his present contract with the United Nations, which expires on 30 June 1971, I should be happy to offer him the important post of Director of my own Executive Office. He would also continue to supervise the work of the Economic and Social Council Secretariat until we have been able to find a suitable replacement for him.

Mwalimu sent the following reply to U Thant in a letter dated 5 January 1970, with a copy to me:

On my return to Dar-es-Salaam from an up-country safari, I recently received your letter of 12th December, 1969, relating to a possible further United Nations appointment for Mr. Al Noor Kassum.

The knowledge that you would like to use Mr. Kassum in your own Executive Office caused me to give very serious reconsideration to the plans we had been making. I do fully appreciate your need to have people of first-class ability in your Office, and we are happy that you consider a Tanzanian fitted for this post.

Nonetheless, I have finally decided that I must ask Mr. Kassum to return to Tanzania. We need him here, and I have had to assume that it is easier for you than for us to get another person of his ability. I therefore hope you will understand my decision to ask Mr. Kassum to return at the beginning of April, 1970. In particular, I hope that you will realise that the decision has not been taken because of any lack of support for the United Nations, or lack of appreciation of the United Nations' need for persons of high ability from its different member states.

In the letter accompanying the copy of his letter to U Thant, Mwalimu wrote to me:

Thank you for your letter of 12th December, enclosing that from U Thant.

As you will see from the copy of my letter to U Thant, which is enclosed, I want you back.

I was helped to make this decision by your own willingness, and indeed desire, to serve Tanzania wherever you are required, and at what I know will be considerable material disadvantage.

I would like to send my good New Year wishes to you and to Mrs. Kassum, and to say that I am happy that in 1970 you will be back working directly with us in the development of Tanzania.

I enjoyed my stay in New York. There was a small Ismaili community and we met regularly for prayers at the home of Sadru Devji, an Ismaili Muslim businessman. I wrote to the Aga Khan and asked if we could establish an official *jamatkhana*. The Aga Khan agreed and subsequently appointed Sadru Devji and a Doctor Karim as the community leaders.

After leaving the United Nations, I spent some time in France and then returned to Dar es Salaam. On 14 October 1970, U Thant wrote to me:

I regret that because of my heavy commitments in recent months I have not yet had an opportunity of writing to you formally to express my deep appreciation of the services you rendered the Secretariat and my best wishes for your future career.

As Secretary of the Economic and Social Council and of the Second Committee of the General Assembly, you made a unique contribution to the work of the Organization and did much to ensure the smooth functioning and increase the prestige of the Council and the Committee, earning the respect and affection, not only of your colleagues, but of the representatives of the Member States you so ably served. I am sure that the diplomatic sense, energy, leadership and organizing ability you brought to your duties in the Secretariat will be equally valuable in the discharge of your important new functions in Tanzania.

As you know, I very much regret your decision to leave the Secretariat. However, I fully understand your desire to place your abilities at the service of your own country, and wish you every success in your new endeavours.

5

DIAMONDS

On my return to Tanzania, I was appointed Deputy General Manager of Williamson Diamonds Ltd., in which the government had a 50 per cent share, with the rest being owned by De Beers of South Africa.

The mine had an interesting history. The first Tanganyika diamond was found in 1911, and commercial production began in 1925. However, diamond mining was carried out only on a small scale until a Canadian geologist, Dr John T. Williamson, discovered a diamond deposit at Mwadui in the Shinyanga area, and registered a claim on 9 March 1940. Williamson had worked for Anglo-American Corporation in Tanganyika, carrying out geological explorations near the company's small diamond mines in the Shinyanga area until 1938, when Anglo-American closed its Tanganyika diamond operations. Instead of continuing with the company, he decided to stay on in Tanganyika and took a mining lease on diamond workings formerly held by Anglo-American at Kizimbi.

Unable to find any diamonds, he obtained a loan from another prospector and negotiated supplies on credit from a shopkeeper and then, together with his Tanganyikan assistant Bundallah, started searching for diamonds over a wider area. On 6 March 1940, with the money having almost run out, Bundallah found small nodules of ilmenite, which is a guide to the kimberlite rock in which diamonds are found. He collected a sample of the soil and walked the 30 km back to their base, arriving that evening. He and Williamson washed and screened the sample that same night, coming up with a 2-carat gem-quality diamond. Follow-up sampling showed the site of the find to be part of a diamondiferous kimberlite pipe covering 1.5 square kilometres. It was the largest such pipe ever found.

The Williamson mine at Mwadui yielded both gem-quality stones as well as industrial diamonds. The onset of the Second World War made a dependable source of industrial diamonds very important to Britain, so Williamson Diamonds was given financial and logistical support by the colonial government. In 1947, a 54-carat rose-pink gem-quality stone from Mwadui was cut into a 26.6-carat brooch and presented as a wedding gift to Princess (now Queen) Elizabeth. Large-scale production was achieved in 1951 and Tanzania's largest diamond, weighing 241 carats, was found at the Mwadui mine in 1956.

Williamson owned two-thirds of the shares in Williamson Diamonds Ltd., the rest being owned by two other people. Bundallah also benefited financially from the success of the enterprise and retired in very comfortable circumstances. When Williamson wanted exploration rights for other parcels of land, he agreed that the (then British colonial) government would have the right to approve any future sale of the mine. On his death on 8 January 1958, his will left his property almost entirely to his family. They informed the government that they wished to keep the mine in the family and that they wanted to pay the estate duty in cash.

However, in June 1958 De Beers Consolidated Mines Ltd., the international diamond company based in South Africa, informed the government that they had been approached by the Williamson directors to make an offer for the mine and requested approval of the sale agreement, under which De Beers undertook to pay the outstanding estate duty on Dr. Williamson's share of the company. The government then undertook lengthy negotiations with De Beers and the directors, culminating in the government receiving 320 shares as estate duty on the property left by Williamson and buying another 280 shares from De Beers for the same price at which De Beers had bought them from the company directors. This total of 600 shares was equivalent to 50 per cent of the company. Financially, this meant that the government would benefit in several ways.

Located at Mwadui, Shinyanga, Williamson Diamonds employed almost 3,000 people. In 1969 it sold diamonds worth about Shs. 156 million, out of which about Shs. 52 million went to the government in the form of royalties, the diamond levy and tax. In addition, the government, through the National Development Corporation, received Shs. 19 million in dividends. However, in spite of the joint ownership, the top management of Williamson Diamonds were all South African or English – not a single Tanzanian until my appointment as Deputy General Manager.

When Mwalimu told me what he had in mind, I was surprised and said: 'But I am a lawyer! I have done all these international jobs. I have worked in my father's shop, sliced meat, kept godowns, cleared goods from customs. I don't know anything about diamonds!' He said, 'Don't worry, just go there, stay for a while, let's see what happens. I just want you to go there.' I said, 'All right, if that is what you want.' Mwalimu said he wanted me to find out what was going on at the company since it was being very secretive about its operations.

At Williamson Diamonds, I was given an impressive office next door to the Managing Director, George Hunt. He threw a welcome party for me, at which I was introduced to his wife and his mother. I was made a member of the tennis club. There were parties, we went dancing, we played tennis, we swam, we took part in many leisure activities. And, of course, I was shown around the mine and the sorting house.

Right from the beginning, however, the company executives tried to sideline me where management was concerned. Whenever a critical decision had to be taken by the management, the executives met in the Managing Director's office, but I was never invited. It was obvious that I would have to find other ways of obtaining information. So I made friends with all their wives. I was a very good dancer. I went to parties and chatted with the wives on the dance floor; and visited the husbands at home and in their offices to get them into conversations about the business. They controlled various parts of the business – some in sorting, some in valuation, some in sizing the diamonds, and so on – and they liked showing off their expertise to me.

Over a year, I compiled a considerable amount of information on the diamond mine. I also attended the annual general meeting, where I was able to get more information. I learned that after the diamonds had been mined, sized and valued, they were sent to the Tanzania Diamond Sorting Office in London for further sorting. Then they were sent to De Beers, which had a virtual monopoly over the international diamond trade. De Beers bought stones from most of the diamond producers all over the world and they were sorted into little packages containing particular types of diamonds in accordance with their customers' needs. Once a year, buyers would be invited to come and purchase the diamonds. This arrangement enabled De Beers to control supply and thus the international diamond price. If there was a surplus, De Beers would hoard it to ensure that the price did not fall.

In Tanzania, De Beers tried to ensure that it would control not only the current mine but also potential mines. They bought concessionary rights over several areas that had the right sort of geology for diamond production, but did not then go on to investigate whether diamonds did actually exist there. The result was that no one else had access to those sites. Tanzanians who had been trained in the diamond trade were sent by De Beers to Botswana instead of being employed in Tanzania. It is only recently that some of those concessions in Tanzania began to be explored.

I asked the National Development Corporation (NDC), which was the formal owner of the government's shares in Williamson Diamonds, for help with statistics such as the number of people working at Williamson Diamonds, the sales reported officially, and so on. As half-owner, NDC, of course, had access to such information. The information was provided to me by Basil Mramba, who was later appointed Tanzania's Minister of Finance. He also helped with the writing of my report.

The report, titled 'The Future of Mwadui', gave details of the Williamson Diamonds operations. It was divided into three parts. The first part focused on reduction of working costs, the second contained a cost-benefit analysis of the mine's operations under various scenarios, and the third presented suggestions for future uses of the Mwadui Complex.

It noted that the mine had a serious security problem, with the Mwadui police being unable to prevent quality stones being 'creamed off' through theft before marketing. The Canadian government had sent a group of experienced Royal Canadian Mounted Police under a technical assistance programme, and that was expected to have a significant impact on the security problem. There had also been a steady increase in production as well as overhead costs. At the head office, 75 per cent of the 1971 expenditure was attributable to the senior expatriate staff. The report observed that 'when fully localised, this will be reduced to some 25 per cent of the 1971 level'. It also made other suggestions for cost reductions, among them reduction of the company's aircraft and rationalized use of the remaining ones. Under the proposed programme of reductions, costs were expected to fall by a total of about 30 per cent by the end of 1975 – that is, over four years.

The report recommended that the proposed cost reduction and control programme be accepted; specific officers within Williamson Diamonds Ltd. and the National Development Corporation be charged with the development, implementation, monitoring and control of the cost reduction and control programme; detailed action programmes for each cost area, based on the proposed overall action programmes, be immediately developed; the detailed action programme for 1972 be immediately incorporated into the Williamson Diamonds 1972 budget; and a monitoring and control system, based upon the existing computerized Working Account Budgeting and Costing Report, be developed and implemented.

The section on cost reduction ended, 'By the end of 1972 the proposed Cost Reduction and Control Programme should be in full operation. At that time it should be possible to again consider the cost areas that have been excluded from the proposed programme with the object of including them in an enlarged programme.'

The cost-benefit analysis in the second section of the report examined, *inter alia*, the overall economic and financial benefits generated by mining the diamond reserves at different depletion rates over different time periods. The following benefits were calculated: total sales revenue, net cash flows (that is, profits after tax, minus capital expenditures, minus increases in working capital), government royalties and levies, foreign exchange surpluses (sale revenue, minus the overseas cost of imported purchases and finance that returned abroad), and total investible surpluses (the total of all direct surplus plus taxation and duties retained by Tanzania). Four plans were considered: for three years, five years, seven years and ten years. The report concluded that the seven-year plan provided the best overall economic benefits in the longer term. It also advised against any policy of mining the richer ores as soon as possible to generate high sales revenue quickly:

There is one inherent disadvantage of the overmining policy. That is that it results in rapid depletion of the rich ore reserves. This would be entirely acceptable if the reserves were known with certainty. Unfortunately, this is not the case. It is quite likely that within twelve months, much better estimates of the reserves, grades and prices will be available. If these revised estimates differ substantially from those upon which this analysis is based, the mining policy will require revision.

For example, if the kimberlite ores were found to be of higher grade than assumed, it is possible that a longer term policy would be financially and economically justified. Similarly, if the grades were shown to be lower, it may be possible to still maintain the seven-year policy but on a lower revenue basis.

The ability to make such policy changes in twelve months' time depends upon the existence of sufficient quantities of high-grade ore. If, during this time, an overmining policy has been adopted then a disproportionately high level of the richer ores would have been depleted. This could well lead to the situation where there would not be an opportunity to extend the life of the mine, if upward revision of kimberlite grades occurred. Similarly, it may become necessary to change to a five-year policy, if the opposite revision occurred.

To retain the flexibility for future decision making, it is important that overmining does not occur. Hence, the need for a constant mining plan at least in the short term. In twelve months' time, when the reserves are known more accurately, it may be possible to include some element of overmining.

Hence, it is concluded that the seven-year constant mining policy is the preferred choice, in spite of the short-term financial and economic advantages of the overmining plan.

The report also recommended that 'a formal financial monitoring system be set up so that the National Development Corporation can control the financial performance of the business' and added:

The final recommendation is that the financial plan, as outlined in this paper, be placed on to a systematic and computerised basis, with an updating facility built into the system, so that the long-term plan can be revised every six months if necessary. The prime objective of this facility would be to use the latest available information as early as possible, to increase the opportunity of extending the useful economic operating life of the mine.

Over the years, the Mwadui complex had developed its own services for housing, water, electricity, transport, mail, telecommunications, education, health, and so on for its workforce and their families. As a result, it had become a small town, with a population of 8,634 people at the beginning of 1972. The mine had, among other things, its own primary school, training centre, agricultural school, hospitals, power station, water treatment and delivery system, sewerage collection and disposal system, dairy farm (with high-grade Friesian and Jersey cattle) and piggery. Nearby was the Government Shinyanga Secondary School. Therefore, the third part of the report recommended formal development of Mwadui into a major town:

> The potential of developing Mwadui as a major town in Shinyanga region is thought to be considerable. This would require the reallocation of essential services to various Government agencies and then re-integration into a well-knit township. With careful planning, one can envisage a self-supporting Mwadui, generating economic and social activity whose benefits would be felt throughout the region.

Quoting an economic appraisal by P.G. Hatch of the Economic Intelligence Unit, the report suggested, *inter alia*, setting up projects in the field of high-value agricultural products and agroindustries, which 'will make the maximum use of Mwadui's natural assets of cheap water, abundant land and labour, and power availability, while mitigating to the maximum extent the natural disadvantages of high transport costs, lack of raw materials, and high cost of capital goods'.

The report also observed that building on Mwadui's success in breeding high-grade cattle and pigs 'could contribute to the self-sufficiency of Tanzania's food requirements and to a better quality of life' for the population. Among the projects recommended by the report were a tannery and shoe factory; spinning, weaving and knitting the locally produced as well as imported cotton; manufacture of clothing and other cotton products; production of silk; and a brewery.

Williamson Diamonds also had a wholly owned subsidiary, New Alamasi (1963) Limited, whose mine was adjacent to Mwadui. Williamson Diamonds termed it 'a property of marginal profitability' because it processed rocks that could not be economically mined by Williamson Diamonds. The Mwadui report did not make a detailed study of mining operations at New Alamasi, but it noted a significant economic feature:

> The financial arrangements for Mwadui and New Alamasi differ in the two following respects. By the Development Levy Act

No. 42 of 1965, section 25, a levy of 5 per cent of the gross value of diamonds mined after 11th June 1965, was payable provided the gross value of diamonds in the current year is not less than £500,000. This Act was repealed by the Personal Tax Act No. 30 of 1967. But the levy was reinstated by an amendment to the Mining Ordinance No. 130 of 1968 which re-enacted the provisions for a diamond levy. Mwadui pays a 5 per cent levy because it has a production in excess of £500,000 a year whereas New Alamasi is exempted as its production for 1970 was valued at £375,000. In addition, Mwadui pays royalty at the rate of 15 per cent of the gross value whereas New Alamasi pays 7.5 per cent.

The report recommended that 'serious consideration be given to Government paying to NDC [National Development Corporation] the development levy of 5 per cent which it now receives from Mwadui, to form a fund from which NDC will prepare and implement a programme of redeployment of Mwadui assets into non-mining areas'.

One of the consequences of the Mwadui report was that a Tanzanian, Mathew Luhanga, was appointed General Manager of Williamson Diamonds. The report was not well received at Williamson Diamonds. The company's Managing Director, George Hunt, was furious with me when it came out. 'How could you do this to me? It's really an insult!' he said. I replied, 'What insult could be greater than keeping me out of the meetings where you were taking critical decisions about the future of the diamond mine? You completely cut me off. So I felt I had to find out for myself what was happening. So this is precisely what I did, and if you find that insulting I'm sorry, it's just too bad.'

* * * *

While I was at Mwadui, I was phoned by the University of Dar es Salaam, which was one of the institutions asked to nominate candidates for membership of the East African Legislative Assembly (EALA) and asked if they could nominate me as a candidate. The EALA was the legislative arm of the East African Community, which had been established by Tanzania, Kenya and Uganda on 6 June 1967 with the signing of the Treaty for East African Cooperation. It had a total membership of 36, of whom 27 were appointed, nine from each of the three partner states. I expressed interest and was elected by the Tanzanian National Assembly to represent my country at the East African level.

On 8 February 1972, the EALA was addressed by Mwalimu Nyerere. His speech came a year after Dr. Milton Obote, President of Uganda, was overthrown in a coup led by an army sergeant, Idi Amin Dada. Despite this, the East African Community had survived. However, economic competition between the partner countries was causing increasing strains and Mwalimu's speech came at a crucial time. It was particularly important in view of what happened in the Community subsequently. I reproduce part of it here:

Each member [of the EALA] comes from Kenya, Uganda or Tanzania. But in the examination of these [Corporation] Reports − as in other matters − it is necessary that each member should make his contribution to debate as an East African. This does not mean that he should not speak from his or her own experience − experience which will be based largely on one country or another. It does mean, however, a recognition of the implications of international co-operation.

In other words, each member of the Assembly must demonstrate his understanding of two facts. Firstly that co-operation is fundamental to the real interests of us all. And secondly, that it will only be able to continue if available resources are allocated in a manner which benefits both East Africa as a whole and each partner in particular. For East Africa is, unfortunately, not a Federation, and the Community's activities, taken as a whole, must reflect our separate sovereignties as well as our desire for co-operation.

This will not always be very easy. For each of the three Governments at present concerned, deals with its national problems in a different manner − has adopted somewhat different political attitudes. Thus, the people and Government of Tanzania are committed to Ujamaa, and their decisions are taken within the framework policies set out in the Arusha Declaration and Mwongozo [a policy announced in 1971, to decentralise decision-making to the regional level]. On the other hand, the direction of Kenya's development was defined rather differently in Sessional Paper No. 10; and the economic and social philosophy which will guide Uganda's actions in the future is now unclear.

Yet each of our different political philosophies has its own logic, and its own implications, which sometimes impinge upon matters in which our nations co-operate. And this inevitably causes occasional strains and problems for the Community of which we are all members – problems which external forces often try to expand to crisis proportions by false reporting or exaggeration.

Mwalimu told the EALA Members that such problems were inevitable:

That these problems will occur is something we must accept. But we must work together to overcome them on each occasion. For they are a part of international co-operation, and cannot be escaped by wishful thinking. The same is true of the problems which arise out of the different types of economy which our three nations inherited from our colonial master. For these, too, result in different priorities of action for each of the partner states, and therefore in short-term clashes of interest.

But all these facts make it the more important that at this Session, and indeed on all other occasions, the members of this Assembly should think East African. They have to try to understand the motivation and the problems of other partners in the Community, as well as recognising and speaking for the interests of his or her own nation. For, notwithstanding its inevitable frictions, co-operation between our three nations is of vital importance to the economic development of all the partner states; indeed, we would all benefit by an extension of it into the industrial sphere.

For in fact, although we have a Common Market in East Africa, we are ignoring its greatest potentialities – at great cost to each of our nations. We say that we want to establish a real industrial base in East Africa; we want to produce our own steel, our own tyres, our own lorries, our own fertiliser, and so on. Yet whenever any one of our nations considers such a project, we come up against the fact that our national market is too small to make such production a viable economic proposition in the near future. To produce any of these things as cheaply as we can import them, we have to use modern mass-production techniques – which involves massive capital investment, and consequent heavy losses if we produce for only Kenya, or only Uganda, or only Tanzania. In many instances, however, such investment would be justified and sensible if the output served the whole of East Africa; and our Common Market theoretically allows this to happen.

In practice, however, this is not happening. Each of the partner states goes ahead on its own, trying to interest foreign firms or foreign governments in such a project. And the foreign firms do sometimes agree. After all, their main concern is to sell their machinery to us, either for purposes of extending their competition to East Africa, or simply as a means of making immediate profit for themselves. In either case, the cost of the necessary subsidy will have to be borne by us. So we have the absurd position where both Kenya and Tanzania, in partnership with competing firms, set up a tyre factory, each of which requires the whole East African market to be economic.

If we allow this state of affairs to continue, we in East Africa will be throwing away one of the major potential advantages of our international co-operation. That is what we are doing now; we are ignoring the fact that the East African market, taken as a whole, justifies investments which would beggar each of us separately. And the answer, at least theoretically, is simple. It is the allocation among our states of those industries which need the whole East African Market.

We did try to work out such a system of allocation once before. But although the Kampala Agreement of 1965 was right in accepting the principle of allocating industries, it had a major flaw. For we tried to use the allocation of industries as a means of rectifying the imbalance in the economic development of our three nations. This was wrong; it meant that if Kenya accepted the allocation of industries, she was agreeing to hold up her own development.

Fortunately, the problem of economic imbalance has now been dealt with by the system of transfer taxes, and by the rules governing the East African Development Bank. We can, therefore, look again at this question of industrial allocation, without the complication of trying to make it serve purposes other than the national utilisation of our Common Market.

Mwalimu then came to one of the aspects of East African co-operation that was crucial to its success: the importance of taking advantage of the regional market without sacrificing national interests. His words resonate even more today, in light of the subsequent break-up of the East African Community and current efforts to use the lessons of the past to establish a stronger East African Community.

> What is needed is for the organs concerned to sit together and to consider what are the industries which need an East African market if they are to be a viable proposition. Having made such a list, we can then find industries of equal value and allocate one to each partner state – doing this as often as it becomes possible to consider local production of this kind of manufacturing. Each industry would be owned within the state concerned, and under national control, and in accordance with each nation's economic philosophy, but its products would be marketed freely throughout the three territories. Thus, although one industry would be in Kenya, one in Uganda, and another in Tanzania, all three would be East African industries. And the result would be a benefit to the whole area, as well as economic advancement for each of our countries.
>
> In the machinery of the East African Community now, we have the ability to take this initiative, to conduct the necessary negotiations between the partner states, and to reach agreements of mutual benefit. We should use this machinery, and use it now.
>
> At this point, let me assure Members of this Assembly that I am not suggesting that the task of guarding and extending East African co-operation is exclusively theirs. What I am saying is that Members of this Assembly can help national leaders to broaden the angle in which they consider the problems which beset their nations, so that the possibility and needs of regional co-operation are always included within their vision.
>
> Of course, this does not mean that Members should ignore the realities of the situation. And one of these is the fact that the greater the divergence in the political approach of the partner states, the greater is the strain which is put on our economic co-operation. Nor is regional co-operation always practicable in the time available to deal with particular problems. Such things have

to be remembered, for the fundamental attitudes, problems and needs of each of the partner states are the basic facts on which any co-operation has to be based. Co-operation cannot be built up on a foundation of detached theory; it has to make practical sense in terms of our past experience and future aspirations.

Let us, therefore, not underestimate the difficulties which are involved in East African co-operation. But I believe they can be overcome if we all determine to overcome them. For despite all our differences, the peoples of our three nations have much in common – historically, culturally and economically. And in particular, we are all aiming at one thing; that is, the greater development and the greater prosperity of our peoples.

At its lowest, this common objective means that all of our nations are interested in the efficiency and the progress of the Community's activities, and in the well-being of our Common Services; and all of the Corporations of East Africa are publicly owned – they are owned by our three Governments as representatives of our three peoples. Thus, whether we favour private investment or public investment as a means of domestic progress is irrelevant to the Common Services. We all have a vital interest in the success of the Airways, the Railways, the Harbours, and the Posts and Telecommunications, which we own. On these matters there should be no basic differences between East Africans. For anything which reduces the efficiency, future development, or the prosperity of these Corporations, is detrimental to the interests of all three countries. This is a fact which none of us should ever forget.

Mr. Chairman: The institutions, and the fact, of co-operation in East Africa have been under great strain since the coup in Uganda – in January 1971. They survived, and it is very good that they did so. For the break-up of the East African Community would not only mean an economic loss; it would also be a terrible setback to the Community's fundamental long-term objectives. These are, I believe, much more than the economic benefits which our present regional co-operation brings with it, or allows in the future. Our economic co-operation is, and to be meaningful must be, just a stage in Africa's growth towards unity; a unity through which we can obtain and defend the freedom of all Africa – freedom from colonialism, from racialism, and from exploitation of any kind.

But these long-term objectives mean that simple survival at our present stage is not enough. We must move forward to strengthen unity for our ultimate purposes, or we shall slip back to the exclusive consideration of narrow national interests defined only in money terms. That would lead to strains within the Community of a different kind – strains which would not deserve the kind of dedicated service which contributed so much to the Community's survival last year. This we must prevent. Therefore, because the possibilities of advance on the political front have receded for the time being, we must work for what is currently possible – that is, for an expansion of functional co-operation.

In saying this I am not implying that economic co-operation has priority over political co-operation. On the contrary, I believe that economic co-operation alone would mean reducing to a mercenary level all the struggles of our people for human dignity. Our real objective is a political one – greater freedom for us all. But under our present Community arrangements, co-operation in East Africa is organised by Governments and headed by those in control of Governments. In consequence, it is always insecure while the Governments of East Africa remain subject to violent overthrow. To counter that insecurity and to safeguard the Community, it is therefore necessary that we should seek to involve more and more people in the implementation of regional co-operation – thus making it more and more difficult for the Community to be jeopardised by a flagrant disregard of its rules.

Since I had been out of the country when the East African Community was established, my knowledge of Community affairs was based on what I had read in the media and chats with civil servants. I had welcomed the formation of the Community because I was a firm believer in regional cooperation. Right from the days when I had worked in the family shop and travelled to Kenya to obtain goods that we did not have, the advantages of regional economic collaboration had been clear. Therefore, I was very interested in Mwalimu's exhortation to the members of the East African Legislative Assembly. I was determined to do my bit for greater regional economic integration. Once during Mwalimu's address, I caught his eye and observed a flash of pleased recognition there. In retrospect I think that was the moment when he decided it was time to give me other responsibilities.

6

MINISTER IN THE EAST AFRICAN COMMUNITY

In February 1972, when the Williamson Diamonds report was almost ready, I received a message from State House that Mwalimu wanted to see me. When we met, Mwalimu told me, 'Nick, I want to whisper something in your ear. I would like you to be the Minister of Finance and Administration of the East African Community. I am sorting it out with the other two [Presidents] and I don't think there will be a problem, and there should be an announcement soon.' I was shaken. Minister of Finance of the East African Community? To be the colleague of Robert Ouko from Kenya and W. Rwetsiba from Uganda? It would be a great honour. (Captain Marijan replaced W. Rwetsiba in 1975.)

In due time, the matter was arranged and my instrument of appointment was signed by the three East African Presidents: Mwalimu Nyerere, Jomo Kenyatta of Kenya, and Idi Amin Dada of Uganda. It was ironic to have my instrument of appointment signed by Idi Amin: six months later, he expelled all Ugandan Asians from the country, both citizens and non-citizens, without giving them time to arrange their affairs, and expropriated all their property without payment. Anyone who opposed the move was silenced ruthlessly. The *Uganda Argus* quoted him on 21 August 1972 as telling a public meeting:

A few Uganda Africans, including some high officials in Masaka District, are in the pockets of the outgoing Asians and the imperialists and are opposed to the move to expel them. One such official holds a very high position in the Government and is known to be the prime mover of this small pocket of opposition. He is attempting to use the issue to divide the

INSTRUMENT OF APPOINTMENT

IN EXERCISE of the powers conferred by Article 49.2 of the
Treaty for East African Co-operation, the East African
Authority hereby appoints Al-Noor Kassum to be an East
African Minister with effect from the 18th February 1972.

..Julius.K.Nyerere........   President, United Republic
                               of Tanzania

...Idi Amin Dada........   President, Republic of Uganda

..Jomo Kenyatta........   President, Republic of Kenya

ARUSHA.

*Author's letter of appointment as an East African Community Minister, signed
by the three East African Presidents, Julius Nyerere (Tanzania), Idi Amin
Dada (Uganda) and Jomo Kenyatta (Kenya).*

people of this country on a religious basis with the hope that he will achieve his selfish ends. The person concerned is known to the Government and in fact the Government has already lost confidence in him as a result of his dirty activities.

A month later, on 21 September 1972, Uganda's Chief Justice, Benedicto Kiwanuka, was arrested by men in civilian clothing and was never seen again. The country's Foreign Minister, Wanume Kibedi, later quoted Idi Amin as telling him that day: 'The boys have got Kiwanuka. They had to pick him up at the High Court because he knew he was being followed, and he was very careful about his movements.' Kibedi said that Kiwanuka was the person referred to by Idi Amin in his speech and that he had been murdered.

After the expulsion of the Asians, I was concerned that the Ugandans would be hostile to me next time I met them. However, when I attended a meeting of the Community ministers in Kampala, I received red carpet treatment. I was allocated a full floor in a five-star hotel. Interestingly, even when I met Idi Amin in person – several times – there was no indication of any hostility towards me or feeling of discomfort on his part because of my being an Asian. On the contrary, he was very friendly.

* * * *

From the earliest days of his political career, Mwalimu had been in favour of East African cooperation for mutual benefit. His view on cooperation between Tanzania, Kenya and Uganda was that it should serve the people of *all* the three countries, not those of one country at the expense of another. This was clear, for example, from his contribution on 14 October 1958 to a debate in the Tanganyika Legislative Council on a White Paper relating to the colonial policy on the importation of wheat from Kenya, which in turn it imported from other countries such as Argentina.

Mwalimu said the White Paper should be examined from the perspective of the consumer in Tanganyika.

I am getting alarmed by a tendency. Recently consumer goods went up and there are complaints in the streets, complaints in the country – 'Why have the consumer goods gone up?' An-

swers were given, some quietly, some publicly, that it is the
intention to protect some future industry. You look at
Tanganyika. We have no textile industry at all, and many consumers had reason to think that the Tanganyika Government
was trying to protect not the future textile trade in Tanganyika,
but a textile industry which is not doing very well in Uganda.
Now, again, we find that this policy keeps, may raise or maintain
the price to the consumer in Tanganyika at a very high level.
And why? Not because of conflicts between the interests of the
Tanganyika consumers and Tanganyika farmers, which the
Government must somehow try and balance, but because of
some neighbour on the border, of Kenya.

As subsequent events showed, this did not mean that Mwalimu
viewed Kenya with animosity. Quite the opposite: he offered to delay
Tanganyika's independence for a year if Britain granted Kenya and
Uganda independence within that period so that the three countries
could unite in a federation, but the offer was not taken up. It was
only later, on 5 June 1963 (with Tanzania and Uganda already independent and Kenya nearing independence) that the leaders of the
three countries met in Nairobi and issued a declaration that said, *inter
alia*, 'We, the leaders of the people and governments of East Africa
[...] pledge ourselves to the political federation of East Africa [...]
We are nationalists and reject tribalism, racialism or inward-looking
policies.' The proposed political federation was seen as a step
towards pan-African unity.

The joint declaration identified 'economic planning, the maximum
utilisation of manpower and our other resources, the establishment
of a central bank and common defence programme, and foreign and
diplomatic representation' as 'areas in which we need to work
together'.

The optimism of this declaration, however, was not borne out by
the subsequent discussions between representatives of the three
countries. The failure to reach agreement worried members of parliament in Tanzania and Kenya, and on 7 May 1964, at a Conference of
Backbenchers, they urged their leaders to federate the three
countries. The resolution declared, *inter alia*: that the federation of
East African countries could no longer be delayed; that Kenya and
the United Republic of Tanganyika and Zanzibar 'must' federate; and
that the Prime Ministers of Uganda and Kenya and the President of

the United Republic of Tanganyika and Zanzibar should meet on the first available date before 20 May 1964, to sign and publish a declaration of immediate federation. If Uganda was not yet ready to do so, Kenya and the United Republic of Tanganyika and Zanzibar should go ahead and sign such a declaration.

The Backbenchers called on the respective Heads of Government to meet again within 15 days of the signing of the declaration, to sign the interim articles of federation, which would then be ratified by their respective National Assemblies before Budget Day or 16 June 1964, whichever came earlier. They said the constitution of the federation should provide for a strong, federal 'Government of the East African States' and should leave the door open for other African countries to join the federation.

Even though at that time I was Deputy Minister in the Ministry of Industries, Mineral Resources and Power, I attended the Conference of Backbenchers and joined in the appeal for immediate federation of the three East African countries. Furthermore, the Parliamentary Group of the ruling Kenya African National Union (KANU) passed a resolution expressing 'deep concern' over 'the inability of the Kenya members of the Working Party to report to the country how far the federal discussions have gone and the difficulties involved'. The KANU MPs called upon the country's Prime Minister (later, President) Jomo Kenyatta to 'dissolve Kenya's representation in the Working Party and reconstitute a new one, composed of devoted and sincere nationalists'.

On 10 May 1964, Mwalimu Nyerere welcomed the resolution of the Conference of Backbenchers and declared, 'the government of the United Republic and myself are fully committed to entering immediately into a federation with Kenya and Uganda, or with Kenya, or Uganda, alone.' He added, 'I fully realise that we may not all be at the same state of readiness to enter a federation now. If any of our countries are not able to take this step with full commitment it is infinitely better that they should wait.'

This was a contrast to the reaction of the Ugandan Prime Minister, Dr. Milton Obote, who told a group of delegates from the conference that many important issues relating to the differences among the three economies remained to be settled before Uganda could agree to a federation. 'If Tanganyika and Kenya wished to go ahead and federate now, Uganda would wish them well, but would not be forced into any hasty union,' he said. With such differences, the priority became strengthening of common services rather than political federation.

Historical circumstances had already created some shared services in East Africa. Since all three of the countries had been under the colonial domination of Britain, they had a unified railway system and post office. Other common services included civil aviation, customs and excise, income tax, meteorology, fisheries research, and various units focusing on tropical diseases and insect-borne agricultural and livestock threats. In 1947, Britain created the East Africa High Commission (with the Governors of the three territories as its members) as the executive organ of the common services, as well as a Central Legislative Assembly comprising ex-officio members, nominated members and unofficial members elected by the Legislative Council of each of the territories. After Tanganyika's independence in 1961, the East Africa High Commission was replaced by the East African Common Services Organization (EACSO).

Now, unable to agree on federation, the governments of the three countries decided to build upon the already existing structure of the EACSO by replacing it with a new organization, with the hope that sometime in the future a federation would be possible. The interim organization was the East African Community. The agreement to establish it was signed by the three Presidents in Kampala on 6 June 1967 and it came into force on 1 December 1967.

Even without a federation, the Community was viewed internationally as one of the best examples of economic integration in the world. As Commonwealth Secretary-General Shridath Ramphal remarked in 1976 during a visit to the Community headquarters at Arusha, the success or failure of the East African Community would have far-reaching consequences on the efforts of other countries to develop regional economic integration.

In its most visible form, the cooperation between the Community partner states was in the form of four corporations: East African Airways, based in Nairobi; East African Railways, based in Nairobi; East African Harbours, based in Dar es Salaam; and East African Posts and Telecommunications, based in Kampala. There were also the East African Court of Appeal, the highest appeal body for criminal and civil cases, sitting in all the three countries; the East African Development Bank, based in Kampala; the East African Literature Bureau; the Directorate of Civil Aviation; the Customs and

Excise Department; the East African Examinations Council; and the East African Management Institute. In addition, the Community had several research institutes.

There were three East African ministerial portfolios, one for each partner state: Common Market and Economic Affairs; Communications, Research and Social Services; and Finance and Administration. The East African ministers were members of the Community's five councils: Finance; Common Market; Economic Consultative and Planning; Communications; and Research and Social. National ministers were members of the Councils dealing in spheres related to matters coming under their national portfolios. The Councils were chaired by the relevant East African ministers. Each of us had a deputy minister.

The way customs and excise duties were handled provides an indication of how the Community operated. The duties were collected by the Community in all three countries. A percentage was then deducted for Community expenses and the rest was divided among the three countries in accordance with the share they had contributed.

However, competition for investment and ideological differences were threatening to undermine the cooperation between the Community partner states. Instead of being satisfied with their share of the Community revenue, countries started demanding more in order to construct infrastructure such as buildings, courtrooms and airfields. There was also a feeling in some quarters that Tanzania was too socialist. This was exacerbated by the construction of the Tazara railway, which gave Zambia access to Tanzanian ports without having to rely on roads that became almost impassable during the rainy season. The railway was built with considerable help from the People's Republic of China after Western donors refused to provide finance for it. The railway was of benefit to both Zambia and Tanzania. At the ceremony to hand over the completed railway on 14 July 1976, Mwalimu recalled Tanzania's efforts to finance the project through its traditional Western donors:

Sometimes we were heard with apparent sympathy; and answered with pleas of poverty! It did not occur to us that the great, but poor Third World country of China would be able to help, even if it was willing to do so. So when in 1965 I first talked on this subject with the Chinese leaders, I was doing so as

The author with the other two East African Community Ministers, Robert Ouko of Kenya (right) and Captain Marjan of Uganda.

one who talks about his ambitions to a sympathetic but equally powerless friend.

I had underestimated the revolutionary commitment, and the internationalism, of the Chinese people under the leadership of Chairman Mao and the Chinese Communist Party. They told me without hesitation: 'If Tanzania and Zambia need this railway, we shall build it for you.'

I must admit, to our shame, that we remained a little sceptical. We continued to beg the West to help us to build the railway. We utterly failed. But from 1965 Chinese engineers had already been doing preliminary work on the project. And in August 1967 the basic agreement to build this railway was at last signed by China, Tanzania and Zambia. Work began on the design and engineering survey. In July 1970 the loan agreement was signed.

Tanzania had had no other alternative, but in the atmosphere of the Cold War the agreement with China was seen as a turn towards extreme socialism. One consequence of the building of the Tazara railway was that it took lucrative business away from the Kenatco transport firm, in which the Kenyan government had a majority share; perhaps that, too, angered some people in Kenya.

One of the most vocal critics of the East African Community was the very influential Kenyan Attorney-General Charles Njonjo. For example, when contributing to a parliamentary debate on employment of Kenyans in the Customs and Excise Department of the Community in Tanzania, he said, 'If our men are refused work in Tanzania, let us all agree that Tanzanians only work within their territory, Kenyans in theirs and Ugandans only in Uganda.' Njonjo once told the Kenyan Parliament, 'At the moment I am not prepared to board an EAA plane piloted by an African unless I am sure of his qualifications.' In July 1975, he told the MPs: 'There is no goodwill in the Community and that is why it has not succeeded. Most of the services carried out by the Community should be rendered by the individual partner states to their people.' He said the Community should be broken up.

In its edition of 7 July 1975 the *Weekly Review* of Kenya quoted Njonjo as saying in an interview: 'We should each have separate airlines to take care of internal flights in each country. The railways should be broken up too. Kenya and Uganda can co-operate on their rail systems, but I see no need to keep the Railways one unit. And, of course, the Harbours for all practical purposes are running as separate units.'

Disputes arose over how the money earned by the Corporations should be divided up. As a result, the three countries stopped transferring funds to the Corporations' headquarters. For example, in July 1975 the Railways Corporation had quite a healthy balance of Shs. 75 million, but could not access it to buy spare parts because the money was being retained by the three countries. East African Airways was in a similar plight, with debts of Shs. 32 million while having Shs 76 million owed to it. The Harbours Corporation and Posts and Telecommunications Corporation also found the transfer of their money blocked by the three countries.

In February 1974 Kenya took over all East African Railways Corporation assets and services in the country. Railway services between Kenya and Tanzania were suspended for some time and Kenya refused to supply spare parts to Tanzania and Uganda unless they were paid for in advance in Kenyan currency. Tanzania paid Shs. 2 million up front for spare parts but did not receive any. Nor was the money accounted for. Faced with the potential breakdown of rail services in Tanzania, the government was forced to order spare parts directly from the Canadian manufacturer.

The press did not help the situation, frequently publishing one-sided articles based on rumours or playing up inflammatory state-ments by various politicians. As Mwalimu noted when officially opening the East African Community Management Institute in Arusha on 6 December 1975:

On an exclusive diet of Tanzania newspapers it would be difficult to avoid the conclusion that the Community serves only Kenya, and that all Kenya leaders are avaricious devils without horns. Reading only Kenya newspapers would lead one to believe that Tanzania is a parasite on the Community, and that all its leaders are concerned only to damage the economy and the good name of Kenya. Uganda journals have not been altogether innocent of this kind of thing, either, although gener-ally they have been preoccupied with less mundane disputes.

I think all these newspapers and the politicians in each of our three countries who have provided the basis for their stories, have done a disservice to the Community and to Africa by the manner in which they reported and commented.

Mwalimu pinpointed the reasons for the problems being experienced by the Community:

In the Treaty for East African Co-operation our three nations tied themselves so closely together that one could hardly move without affecting one or both of the others. And friction engenders heat! We jointly own things which are vital to each of our economies. What can an African country do without an efficient railway, without harbours which work efficiently, without posts and telegraphic services, and so on?

And yet while each of us was piling more work onto these East African Corporations, East Africa did not have the resources necessary to expand them as rapidly as necessary; nor could we raise so much money. So they proved incapable of doing everything we wanted them to do. Consequently there was a temptation to grab bits of East African property for exclusively national purposes, or to undercut the profitability of the Corporations for national ends, or simply to make demands upon them regardless of the interests of the other partners. These temptations were not always resisted! And then there were new cries of outrage, and new suspicions and hostilities engendered.

The truth is that we in East Africa have been trying – and are still trying – to do something which is extremely good but also extremely difficult. We are three sovereign independent states, each with its own political philosophy and ideas, and each with its own urgent needs. This means that major decisions on all the important matters covered by the Treaty have to be unanimously agreed by three governments, each of which is directly responsible only for developments within its own territory. There is no final arbiter – no single supreme authority. Instead, each of our Governments is required to give and take, and to compromise, and then to stand up for that compromise against domestic critics. Further, we have to be able to convince ourselves, and our critics, that over a period all the partners get a fair share of the advantages and disadvantages of co-operation. And we have to do this although our countries are all poor, but still at different levels of economic advance, with different amounts of past East African investment secured within each territory.

Referring to allegations reported by some of the media, that Tanzania wanted to break up the Community so that it could replace it with cooperation with Mozambique and Zambia, Mwalimu said:

> Of course Tanzania is anxious to co-operate with her Southern neighbours – as, I presume, Kenya and Uganda are with their other neighbours. Indeed, I myself still believe that our Community would be strengthened if it were expanded to include any of East Africa's neighbours who are willing to join. [...]
>
> When our three countries established the East African Community, we all expressed the hope that it would be a beginning of wider co-operation. Those who try to suggest that Tanzania wants to break up the Community so as to co-operate with other African nations are – to put it slightly mildly – talking through their hat – if they wear any hats.

The Community was especially affected by the dissolution of the Income Tax Department. Income tax had become a central instrument of fiscal policy only after independence, when the three countries made development in all its facets a priority. As the indigenous populations advanced from a subsistence economy to a monetary one, the tax base in East Africa widened and the collection of income tax increased from Shs. 426.6 million in 1962/63 to Shs. 1,609 million in 1971/72 – a growth of 377 per cent over nine years. In accordance with the 1967 Treaty for East African Cooperation, the Department was gradually decentralized, so that most of the tax was collected by the regional offices and the State Commissioners were given substantial powers. The contributions to the General Fund Services, through which all the Community services except corporations were financed, were made from the capital cities of the three countries rather than from the head office of the Department.

Over the years, the Income Tax Department began to be criticized for inefficiencies arising out of shortage of highly qualified personnel, ambiguities in the Treaty over the precise nature of decentralization, and accommodation of national concerns through many drastic amendments to the Income Tax (Management) Act. Also, the partner states introduced personal tax systems, which varied from country to country. The result was that individuals were being taxed by two organs on the same source of income, leading to administrative duplication and inconvenience to taxpayers.

In 1970, the Finance Council of the Community decided to invite the International Monetary Fund (IMF) to send a mission to review the tax system in East Africa. However, the invitation was deferred in 1971 at the request of the Tanzania government. In January 1972, Kenya announced that it had requested the IMF to send a mission to review its tax system. The Finance Council then decided that the mission should also visit the other two partner states. On 4 April 1973, the Finance Ministers of the three countries informed the Finance Council meeting, which I was chairing, that they had agreed to the establishment of national income tax institutions. However, there had been no agreement on how the Community's operations would be financed. At a later meeting it was agreed that the partner states would continue to contribute their share to the Community, and that their contribution would be deducted from their customs and excise revenue.

The East African Legislative Assembly opposed the dissolution of the Income Tax Department, defeating legislation that was brought before it for that purpose. Nevertheless, the *de facto* dissolution was carried out and the necessary legislation was passed independently by the partner states.

In spite of the difficulties that the Community was experiencing, I had faith that over time the partner states would learn from their past mistakes and develop a framework for better cooperation. As I told a meeting of the TANU Youth League's Dar es Salaam University branch on 5 August 1976:

Like many others, I accept the view that, although these problems in the Community have been real, they should not make us despondent and gloomy; rather, every effort should also be made to contribute positively as an ingredient in building up our experience so that we do not repeat the same mistakes.

In my view, if the Treaty for East African Cooperation has proved to be imperfect, this is because as human beings we could not foresee everything at the time of drafting. It is, for example, quite possible that several of our assumptions were wrong. Also, many new developments which we could not possibly have foreseen at the time of the Treaty have taken place in East Africa. This, after all, is to be expected in young developing countries and is at the same time the essence of a dynamic situation.

It was while I was the East African Minister for Finance and Administration that the new Community headquarters in Arusha were built. I was instrumental in raising the finance for it, through negotiations with the Societé Condotte d'Aqua, an Italian financial institution in which the Vatican held 50 per cent of the shares. The Societé Condotte d'Aqua agreed to lend the required amount if the governments of Tanzania, Kenya and Uganda guaranteed the loan. This presented a problem because the Community's principal executive authority, comprising the Presidents of the three countries, had stopped holding regular meetings because Mwalimu Nyerere refused to recognize Idi Amin as President of Uganda.

The guarantee was first signed on behalf of Tanzania by the Finance Minister, Cleopa Msuya. Kenya's Minister for Finance, Mwai Kibaki, told me that he would be able to sign the guarantee on behalf of his country only after the proposal had been tabled in Parliament and no objection had been raised to it over a period of ten days. During those ten days I stayed at a hotel in Nairobi. When the time was up, Kibaki called me and said no objection had been raised in Parliament, so I went to the Ministry and Kibaki signed and sealed the document in front of me. Uganda presented a tougher hurdle. The agreement by the three East African leaders to build the Community headquarters had been signed when Milton Obote was in power, and Idi Amin's Minister for Finance was reluctant to sign the loan guarantee on that basis. After a lengthy discussion, he agreed that, in the interests of maintaining the Community and its various activities, it would be correct for him to sign the agreement, and he did so. Unfortunately, he did not have a government seal with him, so I suggested he should just stamp it with a rubber stamp specifying his name and ministerial position. He did so, and the Societé Condotte d'Aqua accepted the loan guarantee on that basis. We signed the agreement on 22 September 1972 and began the construction of the Community headquarters and other associated buildings.

There was no way to get the three Presidents together to lay the foundation stone, but I held my own personal dedication ceremony. One night I went with my family and friends to the construction site, where I dug a hole and placed a candle in it. After lighting the candle, we prayed for several minutes and then buried it. Ironically, construction was completed in March 1977, the year that the Community collapsed.

After the break-up of the Community, the building became the Arusha International Conference Centre (AICC), a government-owned commercial enterprise. The building's modern facilities for simultaneous interpretation in several languages and rooms that could cater for small as well as large gatherings made it particularly suitable for this purpose. With Mount Kilimanjaro and three internationally famous wildlife parks (Ngorongoro, Serengeti and Lake Manyara) not too far away, the AICC enjoyed a unique advantage in attracting many international conferences. Conference delegates were able to combine meetings with game park tours. Arusha is served by the Kilimanjaro International Airport, so the delegates could fly in directly. Part of the building was also rented out as office space. Since the modest revival of the East African Community in November 1999 the building once again houses the Community secretariat. Other tenants include the United Nations War Crimes Tribunal for Rwanda; the Commonwealth Regional Health Community Secretariat for East, Central and Southern Africa; and international and Tanzanian private-sector companies.

In 1975, while I was the East African Minister for Finance and Administration, the United Nations invited me to chair a group of 25 experts evaluating how the United Nations system could be restructured, following a UN resolution on the New World Economic Order. After the report had been submitted to the UN Secretary-General Kurt Waldheim, a workshop was held to discuss it, where the panellists included Kurt Waldheim and U.S. Senator Edward Kennedy. The report was then placed before the UN General Assembly.

Among its recommendations was the appointment of a Deputy Secretary-General of the United Nations, whose portfolio would be economic and social affairs. However, instead of doing this, Waldheim created a new, high-level directorate for economic and social affairs and appointed a Ghanaian, Kenneth Dadzie, to head it. In theory, this made Dadzie second in the UN system. In practice, however, he was not given much power; even when Waldheim was away, the meetings of the Administrative Committee on Co-ordination were chaired by one of the Directors-General instead of by Dadzie. Later, Dadzie was appointed Director-General of the United Nations Conference on Trade and Development.

I believe that the collapse of the East African Community could have been avoided. In broad terms, what East Africa needed was a

The author, with UN Secretary-General Kurt Waldheim, Richard Gardner and US Senator Edward Kennedy at a UN workshop to discuss the report on how the United Nations system could be restructured.

joint industrial strategy aimed at increasing output in the three countries and promoting complementarity; and an interstate monetary arrangement capable of sustaining more interstate trade and accommodating smooth interstate transfer of funds.

Specifically, the integration activities in East Africa had to be intensified through trade, pooling of natural resources and coordinated planning. In the area of trade, markets had to be pooled and the common market strengthened to facilitate exploitation of economies of scale and industrial rationalization. Similarly, external economic bargaining power had to be pooled through joint actions and coordinated policies towards the external world in respect of external trade agreements, export promotion, purchase of technology, terms of foreign investment and external borrowing. The region also needed to seek markets for its products jointly. Natural resources had to be pooled, with the adoption of coordinated development which matched as much as possible the composition of regional demand with the structure of regional resources.

Coordinated planning was a necessity in industry, agriculture, energy and power, and transport and communications. A joint industrial strategy, which could have included the establishment of joint ventures, was needed. Methods of financing and location of industries had to be agreed upon. For example, chemical and pharmaceutical industries, and those using iron and steel as their raw materials, which required the entire East African market for viability, had to be established on an East African basis. The location of such industries in the three partner states on a more equitable basis would have not only assisted in reducing trade imbalances but also generated more interstate trade, thus reducing imports from outside the region. In addition, it was important to distinguish between goods that were truly locally manufactured and those that had a high content of imported material. The latter should have had a common external tariff imposed on them.

Agriculture was an area to which the Community did not pay sufficient attention. For example, a regional policy on diversification of crops so that all agricultural land was used to grow the crops most suited to it would have been beneficial to all East Africans, creating self-sufficiency on a regional rather than local basis. It would also have created a surplus for export without endangering regional food supplies. Food reserves could have been created on a Community-wide basis, to be used at times of natural disaster.

As far as energy and power were concerned, all three countries were vulnerable to changes in the international price of crude oil because of their reliance on imported oil. Each country was trying to reduce this dependence by exploring and exploiting other forms of energy, but on a national basis. Had this been done on a regional basis, all three countries would have benefited by pooling their efforts.

In the transport and communications sector, the East African corporations needed managerial changes to suit the vast challenges of providing regional services. In making decisions about transport and communications, the three countries needed to take into account the optimum benefits to be obtained from decentralization, standardization and coordinated operations.

Essentially, what was needed was unity, a perception that the strength of the Community as a whole would be beneficial to the people of all three partner states. There was no doubt that the majority of the people in East Africa were in favour of this, and national leaders needed to do more to counter the few voices that tried to promote disunity. I am glad that the East African Community is in the process of being revived again, and that there is more goodwill towards it now.

The new Treaty for the Establishment of the East African Community was signed in Arusha on 30 November 1999 by Presidents Benjamin William Mkapa of Tanzania, Daniel Toroitich arap Moi of Kenya and Yoweri Kaguta Museveni of Uganda. The contents of the Treaty suggest that East African leaders have learnt lessons from the problems of the first Community. The Preamble identifies the main reasons for the collapse of the first Community as

> lack of strong political will, lack of strong participation of the private sector and civil society in the co-operation activities, the continued disproportionate sharing of benefits of the Community among the Partner States due to the differences in their levels of development and lack of adequate policies to address this situation.' It declares the resolve of the three countries to create 'an enabling environment in all the Partner States in order to attract investments and allow the private sector and civil society to play a leading role in the socio-economic development activities through the development of sound macro-economic and sectoral policies and their efficient management.

Article 6 of the Treaty makes it impossible for a regime like Idi Amin Dada's ever again to represent one of the Community's partner states. It sets out the fundamental principles of the Community as: mutual trust, political will and sovereign equality; peaceful coexistence and good neighbourliness; peaceful settlement of disputes; good governance, including adherence to the principles of democracy, the rule of law, accountability, transparency, social justice, equal opportunities, and gender equality, as well as the recognition, promotion and protection of human and peoples' rights in accordance with the provisions of the African Charter on Human and Peoples' Rights; equitable distribution of benefits; and cooperation for mutual benefit.

The first Community had no organ whose directives and decisions had to be accepted and implemented by the partner states. As a result, when disputes arose, the only way to resolve them was through the give-and-take of negotiation. In contrast, the 1999 Treaty established 'the Council' with wide-ranging regulatory and decision-making powers. It meets twice a year (or more often if necessary) and its regulations, directives and decisions 'shall be binding on the Partner States, on all organs and institutions of the Community other than the Summit [comprising the heads of state or government of the partner states], the [East African] Court [of Justice] and the [East African Legislative] Assembly within their jurisdictions, and on those to whom they may under this Treaty be addressed'. Adherence to the Treaty is also enforced by the East African Court of Justice, which, among other things, 'shall ensure the adherence to law in the interpretation and application of and compliance with this Treaty'.

In Article 5, paragraph 2 of the Treaty, the three countries undertake to establish 'a Customs Union, a Common Market, subsequently a Monetary Union and ultimately a Political Federation' with the aim of 'accelerated, harmonious and balanced development and sustained expression of economic activities, the benefit of which shall be equitably shared.' Article 7, paragraph 1, sub-paragraph (f) also declares one of the operating principles of the Community to be 'the equitable distribution of benefits accruing or to be derived from the operations of the Community and measures to address economic imbalances that may arise from such operations'. Thus, one of the principal disputes that affected the first Community – inequitable sharing of economic benefits – is specifically addressed.

On the economic front, one major weakness of the first Community was its failure to implement a policy of regional development. Article 80 of the 1999 Treaty tries to correct this by setting out the strategy and priority areas of industrial development in the context of a regional policy. The partner states agree to take measures to develop an East African industrial development strategy and to promote linkages among industries through diversification of production, specialization and complementarity. The objective is to enhance the spread effects of industrial growth and to facilitate the transfer of technology. They also undertake to facilitate development of small- and medium-scale industries, including subcontracting and other relations between larger and smaller firms; basic capital and intermediate goods industries for the purposes of obtaining the advantages of economies of scale (implying a regional market for their products); and food and agro industries.

The partner states agree to rationalize investments and the full use of established industries in order to promote efficiency in production. They will promote industrial research and development as well as the transfer, acquisition, adaptation and development of modern technology, and training, management and consultancy services through the establishment of joint industrial institutions and other infrastructural facilities. The partner states will harmonize and rationalize investment incentives including those relating to taxation of industries, particularly those that use local materials and labour with a view to promoting the Community as a single investment area; disseminate and exchange industrial and technological information; avoid double taxation; and maintain the standardization, quality assurance, metrology and testing currently applicable and 'such standards as may be adopted by the Council for goods and services produced and traded among the partner states pending the conclusion of a protocol'.

Equitable development of the three partner states is further helped by Article 82, paragraph 1, sub-paragraph (b), which declares agreement to 'harmonise their macro-economic policies, especially in exchange rate policy, interest rate policy, monetary and fiscal policies'. Thus, cut-throat competition for investment by one country providing extra incentives is effectively ruled out. Moreover, paragraph 2, sub-paragraph (c) adds that the three countries will 'develop, harmonise and eventually integrate the financial systems of the Partner States'.

In contrast to the first Community, this time round the three countries do not have jointly owned posts and telecommunications, railways, harbours, and airlines. Instead, the Treaty calls for harmonization of policies, regulations and equipment. The countries agree to coordinate their services to ensure the smooth movement of goods and persons within the Community. In addition, as far as air transport is concerned, 'the Partner States shall take necessary steps to facilitate the establishment of joint air services and the efficient use of aircraft as steps towards the enhancement of air transportation within the Community.'

In view of the history of the first East African Community, there are three more highly significant articles in the 1999 Treaty. Article 146 authorizes the suspension of a partner state from participation in the activities of the Community 'if that State fails to observe and fulfil the fundamental principles and objectives of the Treaty, including failure to meet financial commitments to the Community within a period of 18 months'. Article 147 makes provision for the expulsion of a partner state 'for gross and persistent violation of the principles and objectives of this Treaty after giving such Partner State 12 months' written notice'. Article 149, paragraph 1 specifies that if a partner state withdraws or is expelled from the Community, 'the property of the Community in that Partner State's territory shall remain vested in the Community'. Paragraph 2 declares, 'A State that has ceased to be a Partner State of the Community shall have no claim to any rights over any property and assets of the Community.' Paragraph 3 adds, 'The Community shall continue with its remaining membership notwithstanding withdrawal or expulsion of any Partner State.'

It is evident that the new Treaty is a vast improvement on the previous one. It not only sets out procedures for the resolution of disputes that are binding upon the partner states, but also protects Community assets in the event of a partner state's withdrawal or expulsion. Thus, there can be no legal loophole to enable a disaffected partner state to seize Community assets. In combination with the fact that all three countries now favour 'people-centred and market-driven co-operation' (Article 7), the Treaty provides a firm foundation for the realization of true unity in East Africa, as a step towards the 'realisation of the proposed African Economic Community and Political Union' (Preamble). However, its success will obviously depend upon the integrative forces in the three countries continuing to be stronger than the centrifugal or disintegrative ones. The foundation is there, but what is constructed on the foundation is equally vital.

7

DEVELOPING TANZANIA'S NATURAL RESOURCES

In March 1977, the same month that construction of the Community headquarters was completed, Mwalimu telephoned me and told me that the way things were going, the Community was obviously not going to survive. 'You've done so much work for it, I don't want you to be there for the funeral,' he said. 'Come back home. I want you to be a minister in the national government.'

'But Mwalimu,' I told him, 'I don't know enough Kiswahili, how am I going to manage?'

He replied, 'I am not appointing you a minister or a member of parliament because of your knowledge of Kiswahili. All the members of parliament are supposed to know English, therefore you can communicate in English.'

So Mwalimu appointed me Minister for Water, Energy and Minerals and during my contributions to parliamentary debates and in the Cabinet I spoke in English. There was one exception: my Budget speech was translated into Kiswahili and I read out the Kiswahili version. This was not a problem, since I had adequate knowledge of the language even though I was not fluent enough to speak it extempore.

In 1973, the Organization of Petroleum Exporting Countries (OPEC) raised the international price of crude oil steeply, and its effects on Tanzania were particularly dramatic. Imports of crude oil had to be curtailed to prevent rapid depletion of foreign exchange reserves, and hence the country had to take measures to reduce the consumption of oil. One of the major steps to achieve this was the passage of the Motor Vehicles (Restriction of User) Order, 1974, under which driving for non-essential purposes on Sundays was banned. After I became the Minister for Water, Energy and Minerals,

Edwin Mtei, the Minister for Finance and Planning, asked me to review the costs and benefits of the Sunday driving ban 'in a dispassionate and objective manner' so that we could have a discussion about whether or not the ban was having the required effect.

After our discussion, I submitted a memorandum to Mwalimu on 11 February 1978 outlining our thoughts on the issue. I noted that although there had been overall savings of about 7.5 per cent in the consumption of petroleum products between 1973 and 1976, 'such savings do not appear to have emanated solely or largely from the ban'. The memorandum listed four other factors that could have contributed to the decrease in oil consumption, although information was unavailable as to the degree of their contribution: price increases of major oil products since 1973; restriction on importation of saloon cars; restriction on importation of spare parts, which had led to less use of saloon cars; and reduction of the hours during which petrol could be sold.

The memorandum observed that despite all the restrictions, 'the number of cars on the roads on Sunday afternoons is large. Some private car owners have registered their cars as taxis so as to evade the ban while others somehow manage to obtain permits.'

There were two major cost areas arising from the ban, as noted in the memorandum: firstly, the processing of applications for permits to drive during the ban period involved paperwork and time. Also, there were other inputs such as patrolling the streets, which might not always be identifiable as special services for the purpose of enforcing the ban. Secondly, prosecuting people caught violating the ban was a lengthy and time-consuming process and lifting of the ban would help reduce pressure on the courts.

On the basis of this analysis, the memorandum recommended lifting the ban on Sunday driving. However, Mwalimu felt that that there were insufficient statistics on which to base a lifting of the ban, and so it was continued for about a decade.

In the 1970s the petroleum companies operating in Tanzania were allowed to import their own market share of crude oil and refined products. However, when oil prices rose sharply again in 1979 and the companies failed to import products into Tanzania, the government decided to import oil directly through the Tanzania Petroleum Development Corporation (TPDC). Thus, as Minister, my biggest task was to find as much oil as I could on credit. Tanzania had very little foreign exchange, so we could not buy the oil on the world market. Instead, we had to negotiate bilateral agreements with oil-producing countries.

This posed an additional problem because the oil produced in some of the countries was unsuitable for our needs. For example, processing Angolan oil would have required heating facilities which our refinery did not have. Therefore, we had to use ingenuity in obtaining the oil. For instance, after negotiating 100,000 MT of Cabinda Crude from Angola in 1983, we exchanged it and 40,000 MT of residual fuel oil for 80,000 MT of Iranian Light Crude (which was more suited to our refinery) and 24,000 MT white products (refined products). I also led Ministry teams to Libya, Iran, Algeria and other countries to negotiate supplies. My basic message was: 'We are having temporary problems and so cannot pay immediately for the oil we need. However, we do have natural resources and so can pay you in the longer term. Could you please let us have oil on credit?' And they did so.

TPDC continued to be the sole importer of petroleum products into Tanzania until 1997, when the government started systematic liberalization of the oil sector and the importation of refined products was handed back to the oil companies.

On 2 November 1978, the Ugandan army invaded Tanzania and occupied the area around the Kagera River. Earlier, the Ugandan leader, Idi Amin Dada, had declared the area to be historically a part of Uganda and had said he would annex it. Two months before the invasion, he had falsely claimed that Tanzanian troops had occupied part of Uganda and that they were killing civilians. There were probably two reasons for the Ugandan aggression. As a land-locked country, Uganda was dependent on the port of Mombasa in Kenya for all its exports and imports, and Idi Amin wanted to change that by conquest, in the hope of opening a corridor to the Tanzanian port of Tanga. Also, Mwalimu was one of the few African leaders who had publicly criticized the widespread violation of human rights in Uganda and Idi Amin wanted to silence him.

Addressing Tanzanians after the Ugandan invasion, Mwalimu said the Tanzanian army was fighting back. 'We shall hit very hard,' he promised. Rejecting international calls for mediation, he noted that the invasion was a declaration of war. 'Tanzania has not declared war. A mad man has done so.' In discussions within the Cabinet, he was very bitter about Kenya not expressing support for Tanzania. In any event, the Tanzanian army succeeded in driving the Ugandan forces back and went on the following year to overthrow Idi Amin, who was replaced by President Milton Obote whom he had overthrown eight years previously.

At one stage during the war, we found out that Uganda was about to obtain 25 MT of crude oil through Mombasa, and I used my contacts with the suppliers to stop the consignment. That oil was critical to Uganda, and had it got through it could have prolonged the aggression against Tanzania.

In 1979 the Principal Secretary in my Ministry, Frederick Lwega-rulila, a brilliant water expert from Bukoba, suggested that we do an aerial geophysical survey of Tanzania to determine the country's water and mineral resources. At his suggestion, we had already carried out a successful survey for potable water in the Lake Region in 1977, and that survey had also found evidence of large quantities of tin. One area particularly, Kabanga in the southwest of the Lake Region, close to the border with Burundi, had deposits of nickel, copper, cobalt and platinum. In view of this experience, I was convinced that a national aerial survey would be of considerable benefit.

I put the proposal to Mwalimu, informing him that while such a survey would cost us in the region of US$ 60 million, it could result in the discovery of very valuable mineral resources. In those days, especially in view of the foreign exchange shortage caused by higher oil prices, US$ 60 million was an astronomical amount for Tanzania to spend; however, Mwalimu decided that the potential benefits were worth it and he told me to go ahead.

The German company that conducted the survey, Geosurvey International GmbH, agreed to payment in instalments. The survey was conducted with two Cessna planes from 1977 to 1980 and one of its results was the pinpointing of potential economic gold deposits. In addition, the survey identified more than 100 sites of potential uranium deposits as well as sites where other minerals were likely to exist. The survey showed that we were a resource-rich country. We had water, 70-80 per cent of our land was arable and we had mineral resources which could be developed. All these could be the foundation for developing the country, building an industrial base and extending the agricultural sector. The prospect was exciting.

The results of the survey stimulated international interest and prospecting and mining licences for various minerals were granted to a number of companies. For example, in August 1994 Kahama Mining Corporation, a wholly owned subsidiary of Canada's Sutton Resources Ltd, signed an agreement for exploration and development of the gold deposit at Bulyanhulu in Mwanza District. Sutton Resources described it as one of Africa's largest undeveloped gold deposits. Its 1995 annual report said the deposit had 'returned a phenomenal 2 million ounce increase in gold resources last year, dramatically underscoring the belief we had in its potential'. The company informed its shareholders:

> Our resource is high grade, in fact about twice the grade of the average North American gold mine, and still very much open to expansion.
> Bulyanhulu is also very large. Historically, a gold deposit of Bulyanhulu's size is a rare occurrence. Only 10 per cent of the world's gold deposits ever exceed 3.2 million ounces. After this, they are referred to as 'world-class' gold deposits. [...] In fact, we believe the property potential could be 7 million ounces or more. [...]
> Also very significant is the very low projected cost per ounce of gold produced. [The cost per ounce at Bulyanhulu is $125.] By comparison, the average North American mine yields gold for production costs of over US$ 225 per ounce and South African mines are over US$ 300 per ounce.

In addition, Kabanga Nickel Company Ltd., another subsidiary of Sutton Resources, explored and evaluated the potential of a nickel-cobalt deposit with the help of Broken Hill Proprietory (BHP) of Australia. The annual report described it as 'one of the industry's largest undeveloped deposits'. The company reported:

> Despite using an assumed deposit grade that turned out to be 15 per cent too low (as subsequent calculations showed), and using low metal prices, BHP's evaluation still yielded nearly a 12 per cent internal rate of return for the deposit. This is generally a most acceptable rate of return in the industry for this early stage of evaluation.

Earlier, in May 1989, a Finnish company, Outokumpu Co., had delivered a different report about nickel in Kabanga:

[…] the metallurgy of the Kabanga ore is problematic: The nickel carrier mineral occurs as very fine-grained intergrowths in the iron mineral. Because of the fine-grained nature of the nickel mineral it is impossible to produce nickel concentrates at an acceptable nickel grade and recovery rate.

The orebody lies in the depth of approximately 200-300 m from the surface. The ore grades are in the 1-3 per cent Ni range. The tonnage is not well established; however, the target tonnage of 20-30 million tonnes was not met.

Mainly because of the metallurgical reasons the Kabanga nickel deposit is uneconomic and, unfortunately, there are no improvements in technology in sight to change the situation.

Thus, the Finns missed out on a highly profitable opportunity. The history of mineral prospecting is rife with such examples of missed possibilities that others cash in on. With the revenue from the successful mineral operations, as far as Tanzania is concerned the investment of $60 million in the geophysical survey has more than paid for itself.

Over the 13 years that I was Minister for Water, Energy and Minerals, we also developed and exploited the Songo Songo natural gas reserves and other energy sources in Tanzania. The story of the Songo Songo gas-to-electricity project began in 1969, when the Government of Tanzania signed an agreement permitting AGIP Spa of Italy to explore for oil in the country's seabed. The agreement covered the coastal basin, including the islands of Mafia, Zanzibar and Pemba and the continental shelf up to water depth of 200 metres. Tanzania established a parastatal, the Tanzania Petroleum Development Corporation (TPDC) to oversee AGIP's activities. The TPDC became operational in 1973 with the appointment of key staff. As Minister for Water, Energy and Minerals, I was also Chairman of the TPDC. To help Tanzania, the Government of India seconded two experts, Dr Rajwade, an economist, and Dr K.N. Narayanan, an explorationist, to help with the operationalization of the TPDC.

After commissioning a geophysical survey by a French company, Compagnie General Geophysigne, AGIP drilled its first well in 1973 at Ras Machusi, just north of Bagamoyo in the Zanzibar channel, but only traces of gas were encountered at several levels. A second well was drilled in the water to the north of Songo Songo island, where

AGIP did discover a gas deposit but declared it uneconomic to develop.

However, the TPDC disagreed with this evaluation and the Government of Tanzania asked the Norwegian Petroleum Directorate (NPD) for a second opinion. The NPD estimated the gas reserves to be sizeable and AGIP was therefore requested to relinquish the block around Songo Songo so that the TPDC could carry out further exploration in the area. At Tanzania's request, the Government of India provided the services of its Oil and Natural Gas Commission (ONGC) to drill another well at Songo Songo. In 1976, when the well reached the depth of 2800 feet, it encountered a pool of gas that caused a blow-out. The entire rig and other equipment were lost. In 1977, the year I was appointed Minister, one more well was drilled and it struck gas in adequate quantity to be exploited. The gas comprised 90.07 per cent methane and the rest ethane and propane. Thus, it was suitable for a variety of industrial uses. This was followed by the drilling of another successful well in 1978/79. Throughout the period when the exploration was being discussed at the TPDC, Dr. K. Narayanan was our principal advisor. He was assigned by the ONGC, of which the chairman, Colonel S.P. Wahi, had been advising us over a number of years.

As Minister, I persuaded the World Bank and the European Investment Bank to provide US$ 90 million to drill more wells at Songo Songo. This was the first time that the World Bank had provided funds for oil exploration. The OPEC Fund provided another US$ 10 million. The exploration confirmed reserves of 50 trillion cubic feet of natural gas by 1982. Although four wells were dug at Songo Songo, no oil was discovered; instead, the four wells produced gas in economic quantities, which saved us considerable capital expenditure on exploring for and drilling gas wells.

Our initial plan was to use the gas to produce ammonia and urea fertilizer for the local market as well as for export, but the high capital cost of the project (about US$ 500 million) as well as a slump in the price of fertilizers in the world market forced us to abandon that proposal. Instead, we decided that to use the gas as a substitute for fuel oil in electricity-generation turbines. The Songo Songo gas-to-electricity project was inaugurated on 4 October 2004 and was expected to save Tanzania US$ 50 million every year through reduced imports of jet fuel and oil. As a result of the steep rise in oil prices since then, the savings have been even higher. At that time the government announced plans to meet nearly half of the total electricity demand in Tanzania through gas-based power generation.

At the ceremony marking the inauguration of the Songo Songo gas-to-electricity project, which was presided over by the then President Benjamin Mkapa, I was one of several people presented with awards for 'extraordinary contribution to the success of the Songo Songo project'. Outlining my contribution, the Permanent Secretary of the Ministry of Energy and Minerals, Patrick Rutabanzibwa, said, *inter alia*:

> [...] he also supervised the most rapid expansion of the national [electricity] grid network that we have ever seen. When he was appointed Minister for Energy [in 1977] the grid only covered five regional headquarters out of a total of 20 on the Mainland. By the time he handed his portfolio over to his successor 14 regional headquarters and Zanzibar were connected to the grid and a fifteenth was well on its way to being connected to the Ugandan grid.
>
> He thus put in place the basic gas production infrastructure and created the market for the gas. Without these two fundamentals, the Project could not have happened.

His Excellency Jakaya M. Kikwete, now the President of Tanzania, was also given an award on the same occasion. Patrick Rutabanzibwa said of him:

> As Minister for Water, Energy and Minerals from 1990 to 1994 he guided the initial Project negotiations with Ocelot [one of the original sponsors of the Songo Songo gas-to-electricity project, which subsequently became PanAfrican Energy]. In 1994 he selected the original sponsors, Ocelot and TransCanada PipeLines, over their rival for the Project, Enron. Subsequent to that, as Minister for Finance in 1995 he gave crucial support to what was then seen as an alien concept, that is providing payment and currency convertibility guarantees to private investors.

While we successfully drilled for natural gas, we also continued to invite oil companies to explore for petroleum in Tanzania. I led a ministry team to international capital cities, where we addressed executives of the major oil companies. To create the proper legislative framework for joint venture agreements with oil companies, on 23 July 1980 I presented the Bill for the Petroleum (Exploration and Production) Act, 1980 to the National Assembly. I pointed out to the members of the National Assembly that such agreements 'will enable Tanzania to pass the risk inherent in more detailed exploration to foreign investors and ensure that if petroleum in commercial quantities is discovered we will have access to the financial resources, sophisticated technology and managerial skills necessary for petroleum development'.

The Bill provided for two types of licence: for exploration and for development. An Exploration Licence would be granted at the discretion of the Minister on the basis of the financial standing and competence of the applicant to carry out the proposed programme of exploration as well as the proposals for the employment and training of Tanzanians. The licence would give the applicant exclusive exploratory rights in a particular area. It would be granted on terms giving the government the right to acquire a majority interest in the development of any commercial field that might be discovered.

Should petroleum be discovered in commercial quantities, the holder of the Exploration Licence would have a statutory right to the grant of a Development Licence – provided the applicant submitted a plan of development operations that would ensure the most efficient, beneficial and timely use of the petroleum resources discovered. A Development Licence would be granted for a maximum of 25 years with a right to renewal for a period of not more than 20 years.

By the end of 1985, eight international companies were prospecting for oil. They had found only traces of oil, but the geological structure in some parts of the country made them hopeful of finding economically exploitable oil fields. We were being advised by the Norwegian Petroleum Directorate and the Oil and Natural Gas Commission of India. The expert sent by the Commonwealth Fund for Technical Assistance was Roger Nellist, who helped the Ministry throughout the 1980s in the energy sector and assisted me on a day-to-day basis. Professor Mark Mwandosya of the University of Dar es Salaam also advised me on energy matters. Some time later he joined the Ministry as the First Commissioner for Energy and Petroleum

Affairs. After a variety of other assignments, he is currently a minister in the Tanzania government. On legal matters, Andrew Chenge from the Attorney-General's Chambers was a great help. He, too, is currently a minister.

The aerial survey conducted in the late 1970s for minerals also showed us sources of potable water that were sufficient to supply all the country's needs. We therefore used it to work out a plan to provide potable water throughout Tanzania. We decided to approach all our donor countries and ask them to focus on one region each and help us to construct and maintain the infrastructure for distributing water there. That way, all the technology used in one region would be compatible. Accordingly, the Principal Secretary in the Ministry, Frederick Lwegarulila, and I first travelled to Norway, where I was also to conduct negotiations on oil.

Lwegarulila's diet was heavy on bananas: he ate them at breakfast, lunch and dinner. I used to joke with him that the people in the Lake Region were highly intelligent because they ate only bananas. And that the Wachagaa were also very clever because of their banana diet. And then came the punch line: 'Idi Amin also behaves the way he does because he, too, eats bananas!' Lwegarulila laughed uproariously at the joke.

For years, Lwegarulila had suffered periodically from stomachache, and while we were in Norway he fell ill again. The pain was much more severe than it had ever been and the doctor who examined him said he had a growth in the stomach and needed an immediate operation. He needed permission to operate, and in view of the urgency I gave him the authority. I also sent a message to State House in Dar es Salaam explaining the situation and asking them to inform Lwegarulila's family. The surgeon found a cancerous growth in Lwegarulila's stomach. He excised it and I left Lwegarulila to convalesce for a month while I went with the rest of the Tanzanian delegation to the other countries on our list.

When we returned to pick him up, he seemed to have recovered. A year later, on 7 July 1978, I was in Mbeya, where Mwalimu was to open a coal mine, when I received a phone call from my Deputy Minister, Mustafa Nyang'anyi. He began by saying, 'Nick, Fred is dead.' He told me Lwegarulila had passed away. I flew back to Dar es Salaam and took his body to his family home in Bukoba for burial. He was 57 years old when he died. As a memorial to him, we established the Technical Institute of Dar es Salaam to train water engineers. I often wonder what would have happened if the cancer had been diagnosed earlier, and how happy Lwegarulila would have been to see the fruits of his work.

Lwegarulila once received an offer from the Swedish government to send Tanzanians for training as water engineers in Sweden. We only had 20 Tanzanian engineers in the Ministry at that time. Lwegarulila replied that Swedish technology was too advanced for Tanzania and also very expensive. He suggested that, instead, Sweden should provide scholarships for Tanzanians to be sent to India for training. They agreed, and we made arrangements to send 120 civil engineers and a geophysicist to Roorkee University in India for further training. They were the first to be sent abroad under a comprehensive programme of the Ministry of Water, Energy and Minerals and represented about 43 per cent of the projected demand of about 300 engineers required by the Ministry by 1981/1982.

The students graduated four years later, on 18 May 1979. Roorkee University's normal graduation date was 25 November, but a special ceremony was arranged for the Tanzanians to enable them to graduate earlier. Since it was an important occasion in the country's history, I wrote the following letter to Mwalimu, seeking permission to travel to India for the graduation ceremony:

I am pleased to report that 120 civil engineers and a geophysicist who went to India for training at the Roorkee University in 1975 will be graduating on 12 June 1979. I am attaching hereto a provisional list of allocation of the 120 students who are to graduate on 12 June and who will be attached to major projects within the Ministry and also to the 20 regions. A further 30 students are expected to graduate in June 1980, making a total of 150.

These students were sent there under the sponsorship of SIDA [Swedish International Development Agency] who provided the necessary funds, and places were made available at the University in India through the auspices of the Indian Government.

We have requested SIDA to sponsor another batch of 75 students (45 mechanical and 30 electrical engineers) and it is gratifying to know that SIDA has promised to provide the necessary funds. We are now waiting for information from the

University of Roorkee for confirmation that places would be found for these students.

In view of the fact that such a large number is graduating in one fell swoop, it is felt in the Ministry that we should be represented at ministerial level at the graduation ceremony. As such, I am seeking your permission to be away for a few days to attend.

The Director of Manpower Development, as well as the Principal of the Delesta Water Resources Institute, would be accompanying me.

My request was approved by Mwalimu on 21 May 1979 and I was present at Roorkee University when the Tanzanians received their degrees.

As Minister for Water, Energy and Minerals, I was also Chairman of the Rufiji Basin Development Authority (RUBADA). The biggest project in which RUBADA was involved was the proposed Stiegler's Gorge Power and Flood Control Management project. The Rufiji Basin is the largest river basin in southeastern Tanzania and covers an area of 177,000 km^2. It holds over 60 per cent of the hydroelectric power potential in Tanzania. Stiegler's Gorge, a winding canyon which is about 8 km long and 100 m deep, is located on the Rufiji River and the water moves through it with considerable force: an average river discharge of [900] cubic metres per second was recorded at Stiegler's Gorge between 1956 and 1978. In 1979, we proposed to dam the river and harness its power to generate electricity. Halfslund/ Norplan of Norway were employed as consultants to prepare a feasibility study for the project. The study was financed by the Norwegian government.

The study included the effects of the proposed project on agriculture and the environment. The Rufiji had formed a flood plain downstream, in which about 80,000 hectares had been identified as suitable for development under irrigation. While flooding could be beneficial in supplementing rainfall, it was equally usual for floods to cause considerable damage to crops. Thus, a dam at Stiegler's Gorge could control the floods and benefit the Lower Rufiji Valley. On the environmental front, the study concluded *inter alia* that only 3 per cent of the Selous Wildlife Reserve would be affected.

The feasibility study showed that a total capacity of 2,100 megawatts (MW) could be achieved, spaced over four phases. At the end of Phase I (1990-95) the capacity would be 300 MW; at the end of Phase II (1995-2005) it would be 900 MW; at the end of Phases III and IV (2005-15) it would be 2,100 MW. Thus, the capacity could be stepped up as demand increased over time. This would also spread the total cost over a longer period. The consultants estimated that Stiegler's Gorge could meet all of Tanzania's projected power needs at least until 2010. The total investment cost of all four phases was estimated to be US$ 1,382 million. Unfortunately, we were unable to obtain financing for the project. Instead, the Mtera Dam was built for half the cost of the Stiegler's Gorge project but supplied only 10 per cent of the power the other project would have made available.

The Tanzania Electric Supply Company (TANESCO) spent almost the same amount that the Stiegler's Gorge project would have cost on constructing many small power-generation plants that used fuel oil to produce electricity. Wherever large-scale industry was established, they would build power stations. For example, the first power station to be opened after I became Minister for Water, Energy and Minerals was one with an output of 18 MW in Mwanza. The reason for constructing it was the establishment of the Mwanza Textile Mills. Later, Mwalimu Nyerere told me it had been a mistake not to go ahead with the Stiegler's Gorge project. Had the money spent on those power stations been used on the Stiegler's Gorge project, electricity could have been supplied through cables to the whole country and we would not have the frequent power shortages that continue to plague Tanzania today. The good news is that the current Government has announced its intention to revive the Stiegler's Gorge project.

After witnessing the opening of the Mwanza power station, President Aboud Jumbe of Zanzibar asked me to discuss with him the possibility of supplying electricity to Zanzibar and Pemba. The Managing Director of TANESCO (of which I was also Chairman), J. Kasambala, accompanied me. President Jumbe asked if we could lay a cable from the mainland to Zanzibar and Pemba. We told him that since the channel between the mainland and Zanzibar was not very deep, a cable would be possible at an estimated cost of US$ 60 million. The international price of cloves, Zanzibar's primary foreign exchange earner, was very high at that time and President Jumbe told us to go ahead. The cable was laid at the beginning of September 1979 by a team of engineers and technicians from the Norwegian firm, Standard Telefon Kabelfabrik. It was a three-core cable, the first of its kind to be laid in African waters. After its commissioning the following year, the cable carried electricity which had been transmitted to the coast through overhead lines from the Kidatu Hydroelectric Power Station in Morogoro. Zanzibar's estimated demand was 5 MW, but the cable was capable of transmitting up to 30 MW.

However, laying a cable to Pemba was a problem since the channel between it and Zanzibar as well as between it and the mainland was too deep. Instead, we suggested a small power station to President Jumbe. He said, 'Yes, like the one I saw in Mwanza, that one that Mwalimu opened the other day.' We told him Pemba did not need one of that size, a smaller power station supplying 3-4 MW would be enough to serve its current and future needs. 'No, no, I want the same kind,' he insisted. So, Pemba received an 18 MW power station. Later, when the price of cloves fell, there was no money for diesel and there were recurrent power blackouts. Also, since there was so much unused capacity, part of the power station was disassembled for use elsewhere.

While I was Minister for Water, Energy and Minerals, I once attended a conference in Mexico City where I met Moeen Qureshi, who was then Senior Vice-President Finance of the World Bank. We were sitting next to each other and he asked me about the Tanzanian economy. I explained the policies on the basis of which the economy was being built and it was obviously a different perspective on Tanzania for him. When I finished he asked me, 'Why aren't we giving you all the assistance that you need?' I replied that that was a mystery to me. 'We've got a team in Tanzania now from the World Bank who don't seem to understand the direction in which we are going,' I told him. 'They want to impose unacceptable conditions on us.' After some more discussion, Qureshi told me to get in touch with him if we wanted to have discussions with the World Bank on the issue. I replied that such discussions should be carried out by the Minister for Finance but I would inform Mwalimu of our talk.

When I referred the subject to Mwalimu, he said that I should go to Washington and meet the World Bank people informally since I was not the Minister for Finance. 'Tell them we are not very happy with the way things are going and that we will be making changes on our own terms, not those dictated to us by a team of so-called experts.' So I went to Washington, where I met Robert McNamara, President of the World Bank. I had discussions over lunch with Moeen Qureshi and other World Bank Vice-Presidents. I also had a meeting with Jacques de Larosiere, head of the International Monetary Fund, who remembered me from the meetings of the U.N.'s Administrative Committee on Coordination when I was its Secretary. The reactions were all positive. On my return to Dar es Salaam, I briefed Mwalimu on my meetings. I also kept our Finance Minister, C.D. Msuya, informed of all these developments.

The World Bank and IMF changed the team who were negotiating with us. At the same time, in the annual Budget speech, the Government announced a currency devaluation, ending of some agricultural subsidies and other similar measures. All these were voluntary decisions by the Government and the measures had a favourable impact on the World Bank. Mwalimu addressed meetings of businessmen, telling them that Tanzania was moving towards a market economy. Thus, his successor as President, Ali Hassan Mwinyi, inherited the transition towards a market economy from Mwalimu.

My efforts to obtain oil for Tanzania through bilateral agreements with oil-producing countries had an unexpected and unpleasant outcome in 1983. On 13 November of that year, *The Observer*, a Sunday newspaper in Britain, published an article making the totally untrue allegation that Tanzania was involved in a secret deal to sell oil to South Africa in spite of Pretoria's apartheid policies. This was a serious allegation since Tanzania was in the forefront of the international struggle to end apartheid in South Africa. The *Observer* article also alleged that the Managing Director of TPDC, Sylvester Barongo, and I had corruptly received commissions from a company involved in trading in oil. The allegations shocked Mwalimu, since Tanzania had steadfastly refused to trade with South Africa ever since Tanzania's independence. On 18 November the Government of Tanzania issued the following statement about the *Observer* article:

The Tanzanian Government categorically and with indignation rejects the allegations made in an article in 'The Observer' (a British Sunday newspaper) on 13th November1983 under the headline 'Tanzania in Secret Oil Deal with South Africa'.

Tanzania has declared and observed a total boycott of all trade with South Africa since the independence of the mainland in December 1961. All our partners in trade, whether private companies or public bodies, have always been informed that a condition of our relationship was the total observance of this rule. In particular it has been written into all oil exploration contracts, and all trade documents related to oil products have specified source of origin or destination of exports.

Four specific allegations were made in the article, in addition to the headline and innumerable innuendoes.

One allegation referred to a package deal between Tanzania and Marcotrade, which it alleged (a) did not go to tender and (b) which included a sale of oil to South Africa. The facts on these issues are as follows:

In the second quarter of 1983 the Governments of Tanzania and Angola agreed that Tanzania would be supplied with 100,000 metric tonnes (MT) of Cabinda Crude Oil. It was further agreed that as this Cabinda crude cannot be refined in Tanzania it could be exchanged for more suitable crude oil and other products. The package referred to in the article is this exchange of the Cabinda crude oil for oil which can be refined in our refinery.

In order to effect this exchange five Companies, Shell, AGIP, Crispin Co., Marcotrade and Marc Rich were on 20th June 1983 asked to tender. As soon as replies were received from all these five companies, that is by 10th July 1983, a Committee made up of two officials from the Bank of Tanzania, two officials from National Bank of Commerce and two officials from Tanzania Petroleum Development Corporation (T.P.D.C.) met to consider the offers. This meeting took place on 14th July 1983. It was unanimously agreed that the Marcotrade offer was technically satisfactory and the best financially. It consisted of a package of (i) a supply of Iranian crude (ii) a supply of refined products and (iii) the export of residual fuel oil from our refinery. It was further agreed by the Committee to accept this offer and process documentation immediately. This decision was made to ensure that there was no interruption in supplies of crude or refined products as had happened with an expected consignment from other suppliers during June.

Accordingly, the Iranian crude oil for Tanzania's refinery was loaded on 28th July 1983 long before the crude oil from Cabinda was collected – which eventually happened on 2nd October 1983. For these transactions Letters of Credit were established by Tanzania on 23rd July and 9th September, and by Marcotrade on 6th August and 5th September 1983. The effect of this exchange of documents through Banks was to make money transfers for any of the shipments unnecessary, except for minor adjustments in respect of quantities actually loaded. All the letters of credit specified the origin and destination of imports and exports and did not include South Africa.

On 25th July, 1983 a telex was received by T.P.D.C. from a person representing an unknown Company saying that he was coming to Dar es Salaam to make an offer. On 29th July, he made contact with T.P.D.C. and Bank of Tanzania from Embassy Hotel proposing terms related to the package deal. On 30th July 1983, at the Ministry of Finance the proposal was examined. Accepting this offer would have meant paying cash to Marcotrade for the crude oil which was already on its way and making a new arrangement for the rest of the package. It was therefore unacceptable. First it would have entailed an immediate large outlay of Foreign Exchange; secondly the difference in money terms on a total package of over $50.0 million would have been equal to only $175,000; and thirdly it would have involved cancelling an agreement already made in circumstances where we did not know the background or the performance record of the proposed new party.

Consequently, the Iranian crude was received in Dar es Salaam on 11th August 1983, as planned. The residue which was part of the package was lifted in two lots on 2nd September and 28th September and became the property of Marcotrade on those dates. The first cargo was shipped to Singapore for OROLEUM Bunker Co. and the second cargo was also shipped to Singapore for SHELL.

With regard to the second allegation in the Observer article, the refined products involved in the package were received on the MT Ardmore on 13th October 1983. .The following statement about this consignment was issued by the Government through the London High Commission on 11th November 1983:

'Recently a cargo of refined products purporting to come from BP Singapore was shipped to Tanzania by Marcotrade in a tanker MT ARDMORE which arrived on 13th October.1983. On routine examination of documents TPDC discovered discrepancies which cast doubt on stated origin. It therefore pursued investigations and discovered BP Singapore denied having shipped the products and. that the tanker's previous ports of call were Lagos and Cape Town South Africa. On being confronted with this evidence Marcotrade admitted that the products originated in South Africa. Since independence Tanzania has had a ban on trade with South Africa, a fact of which Marcotrade is well aware. The Government views the shipment of this cargo under misleading documents as a matter of grave concern. It is pursuing further investigations and will announce appropriate action'.

As regards the third allegation, since 1979 two sales of residual oil were to companies other than Marcotrade and these involved barter deals by the Tanzania Harbours Authority. During these four years 17 sales were made to Marcotrade (including the two in the package); in all cases prices were determined by the highest rates given in a daily publication 'Platt's Oilgram' less freight differential. In all the 19 cases the final destination has been identified.

Particular reference was made to the vessel MT Five Valleys, which has called at Dar es Salaam five times to collect residual fuel oil. The first time the Vessel called was in February 1979. It loaded 18,000 MT and sailed for Aden on 9th February 1979. The second shipment of residue was on 3rd March 1980. It loaded 18,700 MT and discharged this cargo in Genoa (Italy) on 3rd April 1980.

The .third shipment was on 24th April 1980. It loaded 18,500 MT and discharged in Singapore on 4th May 1980. The fourth shipment was on 15th October 1980. The vessel loaded 19,000 MT of residue and discharged part cargo in Bombay on 26th October 1980, then sailed for Kandla (India) where she arrived on 5th November and discharged the balance until 8th November 1980. The fifth shipment and the most controversial loaded 14,950 MT on 23rd February 1981.

Marcotrade had passed on this cargo to British/Swiss traders with intended destination Calgriari/Augusta, Italy. Since the vessel obtained part cargo in Dar es Salaam these traders insisted that Marcotrade arrange for more fuel oil within the area and Marcotrade arranged to get this from Tamatave (Madagascar) where the vessel arrived on 1st March and completed loading on 3rd March. The vessel sailed for the Mediterranean, via the Cape, but apparently suffered several breakdowns and had to undergo repairs in Durban. Thereafter it proceeded to Mogadiscio where it discharged the cargo. A certificate (Certified by a Geneva law firm as genuine) from Somali Democratic Republic, that is Somali Shipping Agency and Line, is available with TPDC to prove that the vessel Five Valleys actually discharged fuel oil in Mogadiscio.

Fourthly, specific allegations were made that two Tanzanian leaders have had an improper commercial relationship with Marcotrade although it is also said in the *Observer* .that 'we do not suggest that they knew that Marcotrade was dealing with South Africa'. The two leaders have issued public statements denying the allegations and stating that they are instigating legal action against those responsible for the article; the Government therefore makes no further comment at this stage.

The suggestion that Tanzania has been in a secret oil deal with South Africa is so outrageous in its import and impudence that it merits immense contempt. If anyone has any evidence whatsoever for such a statement we challenge them to make it public. Government can only regard this Observer attack on Tanzania as part of a campaign to undermine the unity of its people and the nation's international standing. For nothing could do more damage to Tanzania's reputation as an implacable enemy of racism and apartheid South Africa than the suggestion that this country is involved in secret deals with that state. Yet the only truth in the article is based on a statement made by the Tanzanian Government itself.

If, on the other hand, all the article is intended to dramatise (albeit at our expense) is that even the most scrupulous country can be duped, no intelligent person living in our real world would find the message startling or surprising. The correct lesson to be drawn from that undeniable fact is that the international community as a whole should impose and enforce comprehensive economic sanctions against apartheid South Africa. Simply to make unsubstantiated allegations against a poor country which is bravely trying to enforce its own sanctions against South Africa, is deliberately to serve South African racism by discouraging the sanctions campaign on the grounds that at present a boycott is sometimes evaded.

Tanzania is not and will not be deterred. Those who know this country well, including the Observer, know how serious it is in its struggle against racist South Africa and the amount of sacrifice it is willing to make in the fight against apartheid.

I instructed solicitors in London to take legal action against *The Observer*. When the case was due to be heard in the Queen's Bench Division of the High Court, the newspaper decided to settle the matter out of court. Consequently, my counsel read out a statement in open court that said, *inter alia*:

On page 1 of the issue of 'The Observer' dated the 13th November 1983, under the heading 'Tanzania in secret oil deal with South Africa', the Defendant published an article alleging that the Plaintiff had corruptly received secret commissions on each shipment of residual fuel oil sold to a company known as Marcotrade SA by the Tanzania Oil Corporation since 1978. On page 10 of the issue of 'The Observer' for the following Sunday dated the 20th November 1983 under the heading 'Captain turned down oil bribe', the Defendant published a second article which effectively repeated the allegation from the first article.

The allegation that the Plaintiff received secret commissions is untrue, and the Defendant appears here today by its Solicitor to acknowledge this and to apologise to the Plaintiff for the hurt and embarrassment which it has caused him. The Defendant has also agreed to pay to the Plaintiff a substantial sum by way of damages and to indemnify him in respect of costs.

The solicitor for *The Observer* responded with the following statement:

May I, on behalf of the Defendant, associate myself with everything that has been said by Mr. Starte. The articles of which the Plaintiff has complained in this action were published in good faith, but they were inaccurate in what they alleged concerning the receipt of commissions by the Plaintiff, and the Defendant readily acknowledges that the Plaintiff is innocent of any such conduct. The Defendant has given an undertaking to the Plaintiff that it will not repeat this allegation. The Defendant is happy to take this opportunity of apologising to Mr. Kassum for the distress and embarrassment he has been caused.

Sylvester Barongo's action was concluded similarly. Later, *The Observer* issued the following statement under the heading 'Apology':

In November 1983 The Observer published two articles with the headings 'Tanzania in secret oil deal with South Africa' and 'Captain turned down oil bribe'. These alleged that Mr. Kassum, Tanzania's Minister for Energy and Minerals, and Mr. Barongo, Managing Director of the Tanzania Petroleum Development Corporation had received secret commissions on shipments of fuel oil sold by the Tanzanian Oil Corporation.

At the High Court on (Date) Mr. Aldred on behalf of The Observer acknowledged that this allegation was untrue, and apologised for the hurt and embarrassment caused to Mr. Kassum and Mr. Barongo. The Observer has agreed to pay substantial damages and to indemnify Mr. Kassum and Mr. Barongo in respect of their legal costs.

In view of my career, the newspaper should have exercised more care and checked the facts instead of publishing untrue allegations.

* * * *

On 31 October 1985 Mwalimu Nyerere awarded me the Medal of the United Republic. The citation read, 'Your contribution to people's rights and development by applying your wide knowledge and experience has not been confined to Tanzania, but has passed beyond our borders to other nations.' After listing the various positions I had held during my career nationally as well as internationally, it concluded, 'Your outstanding achievements in these different positions are many and were for the development and rights of Tanzanians and other peoples throughout the world. You have discharged your duties with great patriotism, obedience, sincerity, and selflessness, with our nation's interests in the forefront.'

The next day Tanzanians were informed that Mwalimu Nyerere had decided to step down and that elections would be held for a new

Mwalimu Julius Nyerere with the author and his wife Yasmin after presenting the Medal of the United Republic to the author.

President. Tanzania was still a one-party state, and the sole candidate of the Chama cha Mapinduzi (Revolutionary Party), Ali Hassan Mwinyi, was elected to replace him. In March 1990, as his term was ending and elections approached, President Mwinyi decided to carry out drastic ministerial changes. He dissolved the Cabinet, the terms of whose members were about to end in a short while anyway, and then reappointed some of the former ministers to the new Cabinet. To my astonishment, I was one of those left out of the new Cabinet.

I was heartened by an informal letter dated 23 March 1990, sent to me by the Minister for Foreign Affairs, Benjamin W. Mkapa, who later, in 1995, was elected President in Tanzania's first multiparty election. The letter said, *inter alia*:

I do want to say how sorry I am that you are leaving the Cabinet. We have worked together closely and admirably over the years. In the various positions you have held in public office, in the Cabinet, in the East African Community and the United Nations, you have served Tanzania with distinction as behoves a dedicated patriot. I have always been struck by the thoroughness and resourcefulness with which you have set about arguing Tanzania's case and safeguarding its interests in complicated negotiations. One safari together comes particularly in mind, namely our visit to Iran, where you did all of this with great patience and refreshing sense of humour. In Cabinet I shall miss the moments when you have intervened and hewed a compromise which, though stated with ease, appeared to be beyond the reach of divided colleagues.

Since I received that letter from Benjamin Mkapa I have been singularly more attached to him than ever before. Throughout our friendship I have always felt that he was one person upon whom I could rely to give me the kind of advice and help I needed whenever I was confronted with a delicate situation in my life.

In 1990 I was appointed Chairman of the Council of the University of Dar es Salaam, which was at that time experiencing severe problems because of internal factors as well as cuts in finances caused by Tanzania's economic difficulties. This necessitated analysis of institutional problems as well as reforms based on that analysis.

The next year, 1991, I was appointed Chairman of the National Development Corporation (NDC), which had been established by an

THE UNITED REPUBLIC OF TANZANIA

Red.
26/6/90

MINISTRY OF FOREIGN AFFAIRS,
P.O. BOX 9000,
DAR ES SALAAM.

MFAC/A.100/1   23rd March, 1990

Dear Nick,

    This is not a formal letter; I am in no position to write one!

    However, I do want to say how sorry I am that you are leaving the Cabinet. We have worked together closely and admirably over the years. In the various positions you have held in public office, in the Cabinet, in the East African Community and the United Nations, you have served Tanzania with distinction as behoves a dedicated patriot. I have always been struck by the thoroughness and resourcefulness with which you have set about arguing Tanzania's case and safeguarding its interests in complicated negotiations. One safari together comes particularly in mind, namely our visit to Iran, where you did all of this with great patience and a refreshing sense of humour. In Cabinet I shall miss the moments when you have intervened and hewed a compromise which though stated with ease appeared to be beyond the reach of divided coleagues.

    But I do not think of you as retiring. So while thanking you for the political tutorial you have given me over the last two decades, for your contribution to our country's development, and for the gift of your family's friendship, I am confident that you will soon carve a niche in our society to enable you to continue serving our country. It is with this assurance in view that I end this letter with a literal "Fare Well".

Very Sincerely Yours,

Benjamin W. Mkapa
MINISTER FOR FOREIGN AFFAIRS

Hon. Nick Kassum, MP
Speakers Office,
DAR ES SALAAM.

Letter from (then) Foreign Affairs Minister Benjamin Mkapa to the author after the Cabinet changes in March 1990.

Act of Parliament in 1962 as the vehicle for the industrial development of Tanzania. As explained earlier in these memoirs, in 1958 I
was commissioned by TANU to draw up the articles of association
of the Mwananchi Development Corporation, which was later
merged with the Tanganyika Development Corporation to form the
NDC. Thus, in a sense my association with the NDC began then.
The link became stronger in 1970 when I was appointed Deputy
General Manager of Williamson Diamonds Ltd., Mwadui, 50 per cent
of which was owned by the NDC. Now I was Chairman of its Board
of Directors, with a very able Managing Director and Chief Executive Officer, Professor Simon Mbilinyi, leading and overseeing the
day-to-day operations.

The NDC had set up many large industries, in which it then held a
controlling interest. At one time it had about 50 companies in its
portfolio. In 1992 the Public Corporations Act (which was amended
in 1993) transferred all shareholdings of public holding corporations
such as the NDC to the Treasury Registrar. The NDC then divested
itself of its subsidiary companies and initiated a policy of joint
ventures with private sector and foreign investors to develop
economically viable projects. This was in tune with the overall
economic liberalization of the Tanzanian economy which made the
private sector the main engine of growth. So, for example, Professor
Mbilinyi and I worked together to privatize TANELEC, a manufacturer of electrical equipment ranging from domestic electric cookers
to distribution transformers, which was owned jointly by the NDC
and the multinational company ABB. Once NDC had done all the
work, the Presidential Parastatal Reform Commission closed the deal
as required by law.

While I was the Minister for Energy and Minerals, one of my
major decisions was to transfer the responsibility of developing the
coal and iron and steel sectors to the Ministry of Industry and Trade,
with the NDC as the executing agent on behalf of the Government.
Little did I know then that the responsibility would revert to me
within a few years as Chairman of the NDC! The major undertaking
developed by the NDC in this regard was the Mchuchuma Colliery
and Thermal Power Station project in the south of the country. The
aim was to use coal to generate electricity in a 400MW power station.
NDC negotiated with a consortium of companies led by Siemens of
South Africa. The current Tanzanian Government has announced
that power production from Mchuchuma coal is to be accelerated.

His Highness Prince Karim Aga Khan and (then) President Ali Hassan Mwinyi sign the Accord of Cooperation for Development between the Government of Tanzania and the Aga Khan Development Network on 12 July 1991, with the author and Tanzanian Foreign Affairs Minister Ahmed Hassan Diria in attendance.

In April 1996 I was reappointed Chairman of the NDC. Professor Mbilinyi had been appointed Minister for Finance after the elections of 1995 and I had a new Managing Director and CEO, Colonel Joseph Leon Simbakalia. With the full support of the Board of Directors, Colonel Simbakalia led the restructuring of the NDC which was necessary for it to be an efficient catalyst for development through joint venture partnerships with the private sector. During my second term as Chairman, from 1996 to 1999, some consolidation and retrenchment took place as part of the restructuring process. Another major achievement during my tenure as Chairman was that NDC became accepted by international financial markets. In August 2002, the year I left the NDC, the Corporation succeeded in obtaining credit from Barclays Bank Plc in London solely on the basis of its balance sheet, without the necessity of a sovereign guarantee.

* * * *

In 1991, His Highness Prince Karim Aga Khan appointed me as his Personal Representative in Tanzania. In this capacity I helped with the establishment of projects undertaken by the Aga Khan Development Network (AKDN) in Tanzania. These ranged from health and education to tourism. I also helped to negotiate the protocol of co-operation between the Government of Tanzania and the AKDN, which facilitated the AKDN's contribution to the country's economic development. I held this position until 2002, when the Aga Khan appointed his brother Prince Amyn Aga Khan as his Personal Representative globally.

In 1993 I succeeded Mwalimu Nyerere as Chancellor of Sokoine University of Agriculture (SUA) in Morogoro and President Ali Hassan Mwinyi bestowed the title of 'Honourable' upon me for life. Named after former Tanzanian Prime Minister Edward Sokoine, the SUA began as a constituent college of the University of Dar es Salaam, specializing in the agricultural sciences. Since becoming an independent university in 1984, it has made great strides. At the twenty-first graduation ceremony in November 2005, there were 618 first degree graduands and 60 receiving higher degrees. Of the latter, 14 received a Ph.D., of whom four were women. Of the first degree graduands, 26 per cent were women, while of those receiving higher degrees 28 per cent were women.

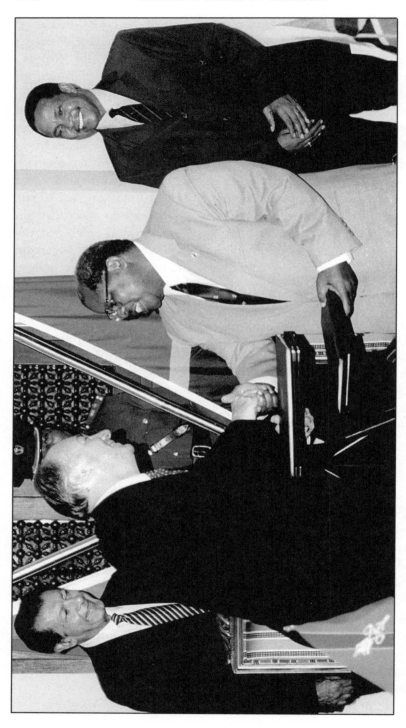

His Highness Prince Karim Aga Khan and (then) Tanzanian President Benjamin Mkapa exchange copies of a protocol for development cooperation, with Jakaya Kikwete (now President of Tanzania) and the author in attendance, August 2001.

On 28 November 1997 SUA awarded an Honorary Doctorate in Philosophy to Mwalimu Nyerere in recognition of his services to humanity and provision of considerable assistance to African countries struggling for their independence. I had the honour of conferring the degree on him.

In 1996, when the Mwalimu Nyerere Foundation (MNF) was established, Mwalimu appointed me as one of its Trustees. The main objective of the MNF is the promotion of peace, unity and people-centred development in Africa. To this end, it initiates and encourages the development of action-oriented proposals for people-centred development programmes and projects based on the sharing of experience, ideas and knowledge among governments, nongovernmental organizations and individuals. The MNF also promotes study of the principles adopted and practised by Mwalimu Nyerere. On 10 January 2000, after Mwalimu passed away, the Board of Trustees elected me as interim chairman for one year. I was succeeded by Salim Ahmed Salim, former Secretary-General of the Organization of African Unity.

His Highness Prince Karim Aga Khan, his brother Prince Amyn Aga Khan, with (then) Tanzanian President Benjamin Mkapa, Mama Anna Mkapa, the author, his wife Yasmin, and other dignitaries at the inauguration of the Lake Manyara Serena Lodge, 18 June 1996.

8

REFLECTIONS

Every morning I walk on the beach behind my house and I see the waves rolling in from the ocean. To my right I can see part of the skyline and a promontory of land jutting out into the ocean. To my left I can see the open sea and in front of me I can see the silhouette of a few islands.

On many occasions I see little children of all races playing in the water, jumping in, splashing and swimming like birds in a pool, laughing, screaming, enjoying themselves as the African sun sets in the evening. As I look at the enjoyment on their faces, I reflect that many of them were born in the last decade. The parents of some may have been teenagers when I was working with Mwalimu Nyerere and a host of others, working for a better tomorrow.

I often walk on the beach at a very slow pace and at times with my walking stick in one hand. As I look towards the horizon, I cannot help reflecting on my own work for this country which gave me birth and for which I have always felt a tremendous affinity and closeness. It was to this country that my father emigrated in the last part of the nineteenth century. It was here that he started his career as a businessman. It was here that I took part in many civic activities and became what I became. It is at times like this that I ask myself: how much did I contribute to achieving Mwalimu Nyerere's vision? And my mind goes back to Mwalimu's own work, what that meant for me and what it means for the country.

When I look at the children splashing around and enjoying themselves with reckless abandon, I ask myself: has the struggle for social justice been completed? Or are we just at the beginning of a larger battle to eradicate poverty, improve health care and increase economic opportunities for the multitude of Tanzanians? I cannot help reflecting that whatever we have done, we have just scratched the surface. The larger struggle for social justice looms on the horizon and people after us will have to contribute to completing the work for which Mwalimu laid the foundations.

Today, Africa south of the Sahara is suffering the ravages of AIDS, tuberculosis and malaria. These three killers are decimating the population. Already we see hundreds and thousands of people dying every day in various countries of southern Africa as well as other parts of the developing world. What needs to be done to enable the millions of people to whom Mwalimu Nyerere dedicated his life to have a better future?

It is at times like these, when I walk on the beach, that my mind goes back to the man who played such an influential role in my own evolution. I remember Mwalimu as a man deeply influenced by his religion and yet not a religious bigot. He constantly spoke out against bigotry, racism and tribalism and took practical steps to eradicate them because he did not believe in inequality. Mwalimu had a particular sense of humour and the ability to laugh at the ridiculous aspects of life. He was the most punctual person I have ever known and that is a quality that I learned from him. In some quarters he was painted as a communist, but that was a false picture. Mwalimu opposed exploitation of any kind and firmly believed that a just economic system should enable everyone, not just a few people, to advance economically. And, in the bipolar ideological environment of the Cold War, that was interpreted by some people as communism. He believed in democracy, not dictatorship, and his speeches constantly emphasised this particular creed by which he lived.

What were his lasting legacies and what will history remember him for? Firstly, Mwalimu was a highly educated individual. Among other things, he studied the writings of economist and philosopher John Stuart Mill at Edinburgh University and taught in all the different areas of Tanzania. He even translated two of Shakespeare's plays into Kiswahili, the national language. He contributed to the betterment of human knowledge, and in the true sense of compassion and giving, he gave of himself to light the candle of knowledge. Educated as he was, he never shunned the ordinary man, and more than that he was capable of expressing in very simple words some of the most complex concepts modern-day society has to live by. He had the ability to explain to a poor rural farmer the complexities of inflation without using any technical terms. He would explain to them in very simple terms how and why one ton of sisal could no longer buy a tractor as it had the year before or even two years before. Using simple metaphors and similes he could speak to his people about complex economic concepts in a manner that made sense to them. And he did it as a brother, as a friend, as a teacher, as a mentor and as a leader.

Secondly, he showed by his own example what simplicity and compassion meant. He never stood on ceremony. He drove around in a small car instead of in a limousine. He did not expect people to kowtow to him or stand up when they saw him. He simply did his work and never thought of what posterity would think of him. He did his work in a way that he believed would be best for the society he had been entrusted to lead. A simple man with simple tastes, he never made material adornments a prison for himself. He was able to look beyond the temptations of luxury and always think of the poor rural people whom he could serve and to whose destiny he could contribute.

Thirdly, with regard to his own commitment to the development of Tanzania, his admonition to the students who once went on strike at the University of Dar es Salaam was very revealing. He reminded them that the University was not an island in the Indian Ocean, but that it was embedded in the soil of Tanzania and was intended to serve the people of Tanzania. And with a very simple simile he reminded them of the sacrifices that had been made by their parents and the government in sending them to the University. The metaphor he used was of a desert in which a group of people are dying of thirst, and one of them gives the little water they have to another so that he can go to the oasis, fill a water bag and bring it back. And as this person goes towards the oasis he decides not to return and thus shuns and betrays those waiting for him to rescue them.

With such powerful but cogent similes and metaphors, Mwalimu was able to make his people conscious of the powerful forces that were enveloping the Third World, especially the inequitable terms of trade that deprived Tanzanians of their proper share of the world's wealth. He himself worked towards this betterment. He considered his people to be underprivileged because of the institutions and structures that had been created in colonial times, which could not be dismantled by unfurling a national flag or playing a national anthem. Sovereignty to him meant much more than the trappings of ceremony. It meant bringing to the global masses and his people a greater share of the patrimony of their countries and the patrimony of the Earth.

Mwalimu worked for the freedom of all those colonies in Africa that were still struggling for their human dignity. It was in Morogoro that southern African freedom fighters were trained for the future. Sokoine Agricultural University, of which I am currently the Chancellor, was the locus in which thousands of people were trained in development skills so that they could go back and contribute to the betterment of their societies at an opportune time.

How will posterity judge this individual who stood for a vision, who fought for a principle and never relented? Some historians might say that his policies were misguided. Others might say that he brought dignity to the country, eradicated racism. He dissipated the poisonous strength of tribalism and welded Tanzanians into a united nation, a nation of individuals but not a nation of tribes. He always spoke of a Tanzania where every individual would be equal to every other individual. My mind goes back to his earlier speeches where he strongly disapproved of the word 'race' being used, whether it was in the form of 'nonracial' or 'multiracial'. This was deep testimony to a man who did not believe in race, who believed in the human dimension of each individual. When Idi Amin expelled Ugandan Asians, Mwalimu Nyerere was one of the few African leaders to condemn the action. Mwalimu wanted to contribute towards the self-fulfilment of every individual, not only in his own country but also beyond its borders. To do this, he had to take some drastic measures initially, because the economic structures that had been inherited from colonialism were too strong to allow an evolutionary approach. Later, having achieved the required changes, he introduced liberalisation policies that set the stage for the policies followed by his successors in office.

I reflect about Mwalimu very often when I think of my own life. And it was some of these thoughts that were in my mind on the day when my wife Yasmin and I travelled to Butiama, to the Nyerere family home, for his funeral. I could not contain my emotion as all my experiences with Mwalimu flashed through my mind like images in a film.

It would be inappropriate for me not to mention one aspect of my life that is extremely important but which I have deliberately avoided focusing on. From the outset of my career after school, I have been guided to lead a life that did not confuse any of my spiritual and other beliefs with those which deal with political and other similar matters I do not wish to dwell on this subject in depth, but let me say quite honestly that the guidance that I have received all my life, beginning from the late Aga Khan, when he appointed me Administrator of the Aga Khan schools and gave me other social and development responsibilities, and continuing with the present Imam of the Ismaili Muslims, His Highness Karim Aga Khan, has been crucial in the evolution of every aspect of my career.

Having seen all these developments and having been an integral part of the process from the 1940s right up to the turn of the century, I feel a deep sense of happiness that I was given this opportunity. And when I see the Aga Khan Development Network contributing towards the betterment of not only Tanzania, but also many other countries, I feel deep satisfaction that in some small way I have been able to contribute towards the achievement of the Aga Khan's vision.

Looking towards the future of my country, I strongly believe that education in Tanzania should be relevant to the needs and capacities of our people. We should withstand the temptation to merely copy the syllabi of universities in developed countries. At the secondary school level, we need to do away with 'O' levels and 'A' levels and replace them with an international baccalaureate, which would enable students who did well in their examinations to enrol in any university in the world. In addition to education, Tanzania's future will be determined by minerals, mining and agriculture. I believe that we have to develop our own resources with our own capabilities. We need to produce enough agricultural and industrial products to supply our own needs. Furthermore, we need to produce goods for which there is international demand, not just those that can be produced easily. This implies diversification in both agriculture as well as industry, without over-reliance on any single export. The private sector is very important in this process, and it is already playing a part in the country's development as a result of privatisation of the assets of various state corporations.

In this context, I am heartened by the current Tanzanian Government's commitment to vigorous action on projects that will lead to considerable improvement in the lives of Tanzanians. Inaugurating the fourth-phase parliament on 30 December 2005, His Excellency President Jakaya Kikwete reaffirmed the role of agriculture as 'the backbone of our economy' and announced plans to strengthen it. Among other things, he also declared his intention to create a national water master plan and make the improvement of energy supplies a priority. To achieve the latter, the Government will accelerate the production of electricity from Mchuchuma coal and revive the Rusumo River and Stiegler's Gorge hydro-electricity power projects.

On a personal level, I have been blessed with three sons who have all done well in life. All were educated at Harrow School in London. The eldest, Saleem, decided not to go to university immediately after his secondary school studies. Instead, he joined the Royal Air Force, working in the equipment branch. After five years, while I was stationed with the United Nations in New York, he enrolled at Cornell University in the United States. After graduation, he worked with the UN Development Programme and the Aga Khan Foundation. He has earned professional qualifications as a sailor and enjoys sailing in his free time. Diamond went to Cambridge University in England, where he studied medicine. After graduation, he was attached to St Thomas' Hospital in London. Later, he went to McMaster University in Canada, where he qualified as a surgeon (FRCS) and then went on to earn an FRCS in Britain. He met and married April, a Canadian, and is now an Associate Professor at the University of Manitoba. He is also head of the 500-bed St Bonniface Hospital in Winnipeg. The youngest son, Jemal-uddin, studied Engineering with Economics at Oxford University before working for a while with the National Development Corporation in Tanzania. He then went for further studies to Harvard University in the United States. After obtaining an MBA from the Harvard Business School, he was recruited in 1974 by the World Bank through its Young Professionals programme. In 1975 he moved to the International Finance Corporation and then joined the staff of the International Bank for Reconstruction and Development (World Bank) where he was promoted to become one of the Vice-Presidents of the Bank.

My life has also been enriched considerably by my wonderful wife Yasmin, who has been a constant source of help. Yasmin had worked in the office of the UN High Commissioner for Refugees for eight years and the UN Environment Programme for one year when I met her in Dar es Salaam. Though she moved to Montreal in Canada, we communicated by telephone. We married in Montreal on 24 December 1983.

Yasmin is highly talented. Her accomplishments include painting, singing and cooking. She has played in bridge tournaments at various levels. She has a compassionate outlook, which is reflected in her work as a Trustee of the Equal Opportunities for All Trust Fund (a charitable organisation which empowers women through increased economic and educational opportunities, of which Mama Anna Mkapa, former First Lady of Tanzania, is the Chair) and Vice-Chair of Aditi (a charitable organisation of which Aditi Chakravarti, wife of the Indian ambassador, is the Chair). She is also active in Ismaili community affairs.

Yasmin has three children by her previous marriage: Dialla, born on 24 February 1966; Shameez, born on 8 August 1969; and Shaffin, born on 27 February 1971. Dialla studied kinesiology in Vancouver, Canada, and is married to Feroz Kassam. Shameez studied graphic art and interior decoration in Vancouver and is a practitioner in these fields. She is married to Nadeen Pirani. Shaffin earned a Master of Business Administration degree from a Swiss university and has a string of businesses.

I would like to devote these final paragraphs to His Excellency Jakaya Kikwete, President of the United Republic of Tanzania, since it would be appropriate to close the book with him. Audacious as it may be, I would like to refer to my personal history with him.

The President first joined the government as a deputy minister and was my colleague in the Ministry of Water, Energy and Minerals. He was an extremely astute young man who, I was convinced without a doubt in my mind, would one day make his mark in the history of Tanzania. And so it has happened. Recently, I had the honour, in my capacity as Chancellor of Sokoine University of Agriculture (SUA), to be a participant when he inaugurated with dignity the Moshi University College of Cooperatives and Business as a constituent college of SUA.

My prayers now are that the President will execute his responsibilities in every respect so that Tanzania becomes an example of outstanding development in all areas, be they social, economic, cultural or political, and in the wellbeing and overall brotherhood of mankind. May the Almighty give him the strength and capacity to achieve a successful presidency followed by another term of equally great deeds.

His Highness Prince Karim Aga Khan chats with Dr Geraldine Kenney-Wallace, President of McMaster University, Canada, and the author after a graduation ceremony at Aga Khan University, Karachi.

INDEX